D0119651

COMPUTERS
AND
TYPOGRAPHY

Monotype Typography

Michael Harvey

Mood Indigo 1931

Sophisticated Lady 1933

ELLINGTON

Sepia Panorama 1940

CARAVAN 1937

Take the 'A' Train 1941

Conga 1940

Brava

Michael Harvey, the designer of Ellington, (the face is named after Duke Ellington, whose portrait appears above), carves letters in stone and draws them on bookjackets where the narrow format often requires condensed, legible letters.

Ellington is a condensed design combining the clear-cut sparkle of a modern face with some of the lively features of the broad-edged pen. The design has a fresh elegance that will be particularly effective in display, while its compressed forms will prove economical in text setting.

With the exception of 'Take the A Train' which was composed by Billy Strayhorn, the titles shown here are by Duke Ellington, all made famous through his recordings of them.

Cover of Ellington type specimen, designed by Michael Harvey (Monotype 1990).

COMPUTERS
AND
TYPOGRAPHY

Compiled by Rosemary Sassoon

intellect™
Bristol, UK
Portland, OR, USA

First Published in Hardback in 2002 in Great Britain by
Intellect Books, PO Box 862, Bristol BS99 1DE, UK

First Published in USA in 2002 by
Intellect Books, ISBS, 5804 N.E. Hassalo St, Portland, Oregon 97213-3644, USA

Consulting Editor	Masoud Yazdani
Book Design	Pardoe Blacker Publishing Limited
Copy Editor	Peter Young
Cover Design	Pardoe Blacker Publishing Limited

A catalogue record for this book is available from the British Library

ISBN 1-84150-049-6

Printed and bound in Great Britain by Cromwell Press, Wiltshire

Contents

Introduction　　　　　　　　　　　　　　　　　　7

PART 1　ISSUES INVOLVED IN THE DESIGN
　　　　OF WEB SITES

How to arrange text on web pages　　　　　10
GUNNLAUGUR SE BRIEM

Computer screens are not like paper:
typography on the web　　　　　　　　　21
ARI DAVIDOW

PART 2　NON-LATIN TYPOGRAPHY

Non-Latin typesetting in the digital age　　42
FIONA ROSS

English, Japanese and the computer　　　54
EIICHI KONO

PART 3　CHANGES IN WORK PRACTICES

Book design　　　　　　　　　　　　　69
IAN MACKENZIE-KERR

Slouching toward cyberspace: the place of the lettering arts
in a digital era　　　　　　　　　　　75
DAVID LEVY

Changes in the relationship between printer and designer:
craft before, during and after graphic design   81
DAVID JURY

PART 4   LETTERFORMS AND THE COMPUTER

Hand, eye and mind: a design trinity   91
MICHAEL HARVEY

Metafont in the Rockies: the Colorado typemaking project   98
RICHARD SOUTHALL

PART 5   TYPOGRAPHY AND EDUCATIONAL
              SOFTWARE

The design of educational software   118
ROSEMARY SASSOON

Learning by design: the role of design in facilitating learning   132
ROGER DICKINSON

Epilogue   148
Index   149

Introduction

This book is intended as a companion volume to the original *Computers and Typography*, but in no way supercedes it. The first book discussed many of the traditional typographic guidelines, and related them to modern technology. It recognised that this knowledge had not been part of the training or experience of the earlier generation of computer programmers and software designers, and that the importance of such issues was still not fully appreciated.

The following words appeared recently in the publicity for an exhibiton of the work of Sumner Stone, the American calligrapher turned computer type designer: 'As the keyboard becomes a more familiar tool than pen or pencil, and the ancient bond between handwritten letterforms and the type used by printers seems about to vanish, what will determine the standards of legibility, clarity, impact or fluency of the alphabets that fill our daily lives?' This statement seems to echo the concerns of many of the contributors to this book as they chart the changes that the computer inevitably has brought to their work. The experience they bring, resulting from their traditional training allied to their work at the forefront of typographic design in the age of computers, is invaluable.

The structure of this book is similar to the first volume of *Computers and Typography*. The emphasis in the first section is on layout, but concentrates on design for the web, rather than the screen in general. The subject is then broadened out into multicultural aspects of typography and looks at the way computerised type has affected other writing systems. The third section concentrates on the changes in work practices, including the education of typography students, brought about by the spread of computers. The making and shaping of letters takes up the next section and design for educational software completes the picture.

There have been enormous technological steps forward in the last few years. The spread of computers has continued to revolutionise work place practices and education. The internet has transformed personal and business lives and opened up seemingly endless opportunities. With all the technological leaps forward, still there has been little progress in understanding how different typographic and design features can influence or affect the user. By influence I mean how choice of typeface, layout, colour, use of illustration and above all spacing can mean the difference between someone wanting to read (in the case of a web site advertisement) and being able to read easily (in the case of a screen full of text) or having precisely the opposite effect. By affect I mean whether the same factors help a person to assimilate the knowledge they have accessed, and whether the screen layout is arranged to minimise eye fatigue or will unduly dazzle and distract. The ever easier access to more complex techniques is becoming an overwhelming temptation for students and software designers. Briem puts it into perspective in the first chapter when discussing designing for the web: 'Does your information really need every bell, whistle and blinking light of an arcade game?' This concept occurs again and again throughout this volume: both in the destructive propensity to distract from the real purpose of educational software and when stressing the need for design students to learn restraint. They need to be reminded that those who are as skilled with pencil and paper as they are with the mouse will be the most successful.

Just as this work was almost completed, an international meeting entitled *Pen to Printer* (Ditchling 2000) brought many of the issues we had been writing about into sharper focus. One point, made by Hermann Zapf, probably the finest letterer of his generation, was that the image of the letterforms must be in your mind before you start to design a typeface. Later on Michael Harvey, when he was discussing his own typeface designs, described how they all bore a certain resemblance because, as he put it: 'that is how I draw'. The line that you draw is made by a direct action of your body, and is governed by the way you move your body. It is individual to you. When designing entirely on a computer, as many students do today, even with the design all in the mind first, that vision will no longer be subconsciously influenced and bear the mark of the designer's personal hand movements.

I suppose this is how it has always been throughout history at times of transition from an old to a new technology. It is a meeting of those who have spent half their lives in one technology, and who have adapted and often welcomed the new, sifting through the advantages and disadvantages and trying to ensure the best of the past is transferred to the future.

PART I

ISSUES INVOLVED IN THE DESIGN OF WEB SITES

How to arrange text on web pages
GUNNLAUGUR SE BRIEM LETTERFORM DESIGNER CALIFORNIA

'Does your information really need every bell, whistle, and blinking light of an arcade game?'

Computer screens are not like paper: typography on the web
ARI DAVIDOW TYPOGRAPHER WHO NOW APPLIES HIS SKILLS TO THE WEB AND TO VIRTUAL COMMUNITY. ari@ivritype.com

'Given the restraints created by today's web browsers and by HTML, typography, as it is understood to relate to fonts, might seem irrelevant to the web. This is not true, although the issues and the solutions are different to those used for print.'

GUNNLAUGUR SE BRIEM

How to arrange text on web pages

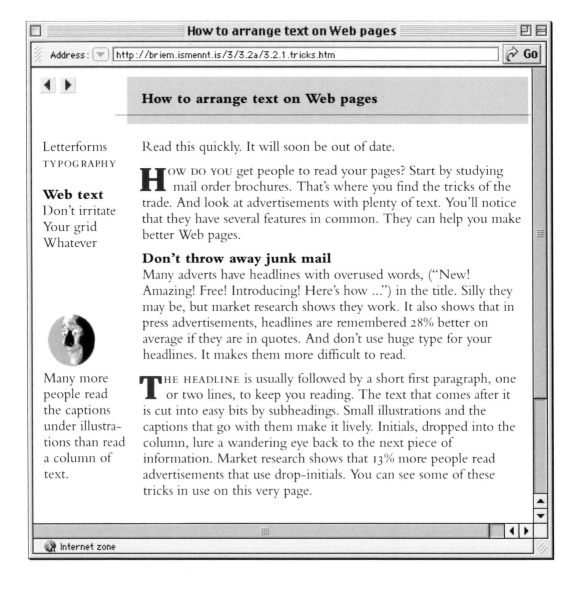

How to arrange text on Web pages

Letterforms
TYPOGRAPHY

Web text
Don't irritate
Your grid
Whatever

Many more
people read
the captions
under illustra-
tions than read
a column of
text.

Read this quickly. It will soon be out of date.

HOW DO YOU get people to read your pages? Start by studying mail order brochures. That's where you find the tricks of the trade. And look at advertisements with plenty of text. You'll notice that they have several features in common. They can help you make better Web pages.

Don't throw away junk mail
Many adverts have headlines with overused words, ("New! Amazing! Free! Introducing! Here's how …") in the title. Silly they may be, but market research shows they work. It also shows that in press advertisements, headlines are remembered 28% better on average if they are in quotes. And don't use huge type for your headlines. It makes them more difficult to read.

THE HEADLINE is usually followed by a short first paragraph, one or two lines, to keep you reading. The text that comes after it is cut into easy bits by subheadings. Small illustrations and the captions that go with them make it lively. Initials, dropped into the column, lure a wandering eye back to the next piece of information. Market research shows that 13% more people read advertisements that use drop-initials. You can see some of these tricks in use on this very page.

Internet zone

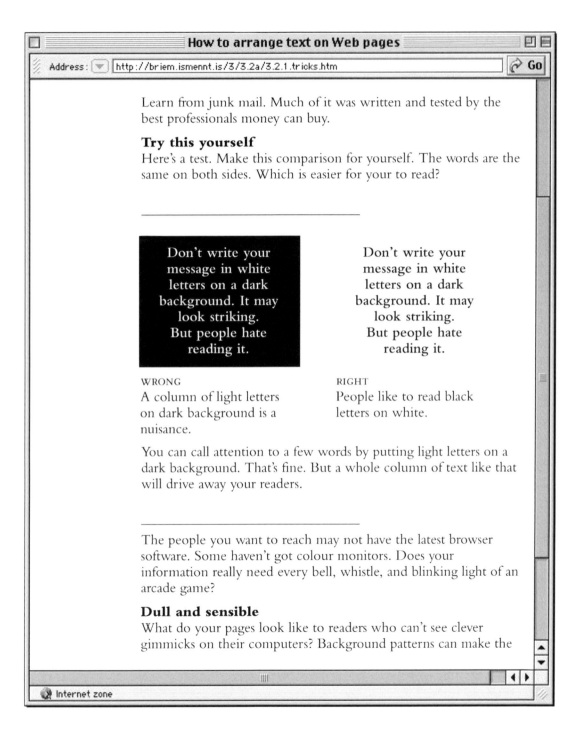

How to arrange text on Web pages

Address: http://briem.ismennt.is/3/3.2a/3.2.1.tricks.htm   Go

Learn from junk mail. Much of it was written and tested by the best professionals money can buy.

Try this yourself
Here's a test. Make this comparison for yourself. The words are the same on both sides. Which is easier for your to read?

Don't write your message in white letters on a dark background. It may look striking. But people hate reading it.

Don't write your message in white letters on a dark background. It may look striking. But people hate reading it.

WRONG
A column of light letters on dark background is a nuisance.

RIGHT
People like to read black letters on white.

You can call attention to a few words by putting light letters on a dark background. That's fine. But a whole column of text like that will drive away your readers.

The people you want to reach may not have the latest browser software. Some haven't got colour monitors. Does your information really need every bell, whistle, and blinking light of an arcade game?

Dull and sensible
What do your pages look like to readers who can't see clever gimmicks on their computers? Background patterns can make the

Internet zone

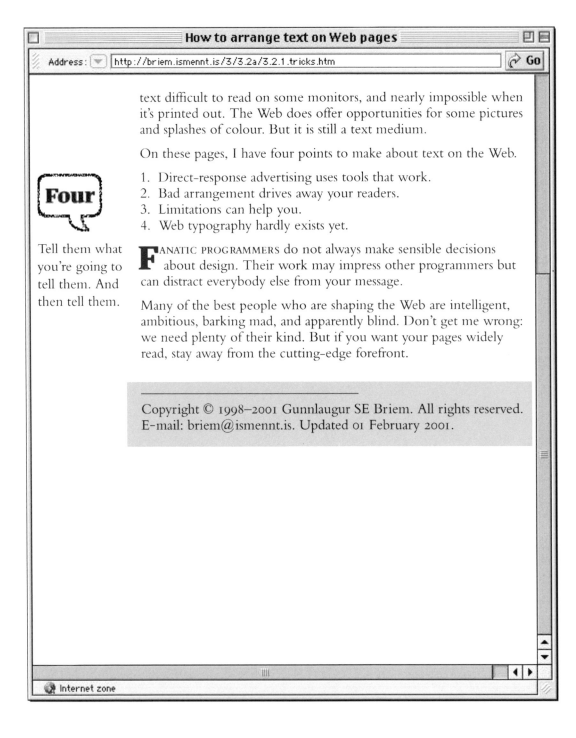

How to arrange text on Web pages

Address: http://briem.ismennt.is/3/3.2a/3.2.1.tricks.htm Go

text difficult to read on some monitors, and nearly impossible when it's printed out. The Web does offer opportunities for some pictures and splashes of colour. But it is still a text medium.

On these pages, I have four points to make about text on the Web.

1. Direct-response advertising uses tools that work.
2. Bad arrangement drives away your readers.
3. Limitations can help you.
4. Web typography hardly exists yet.

Tell them what you're going to tell them. And then tell them.

FANATIC PROGRAMMERS do not always make sensible decisions about design. Their work may impress other programmers but can distract everybody else from your message.

Many of the best people who are shaping the Web are intelligent, ambitious, barking mad, and apparently blind. Don't get me wrong: we need plenty of their kind. But if you want your pages widely read, stay away from the cutting-edge forefront.

Internet zone

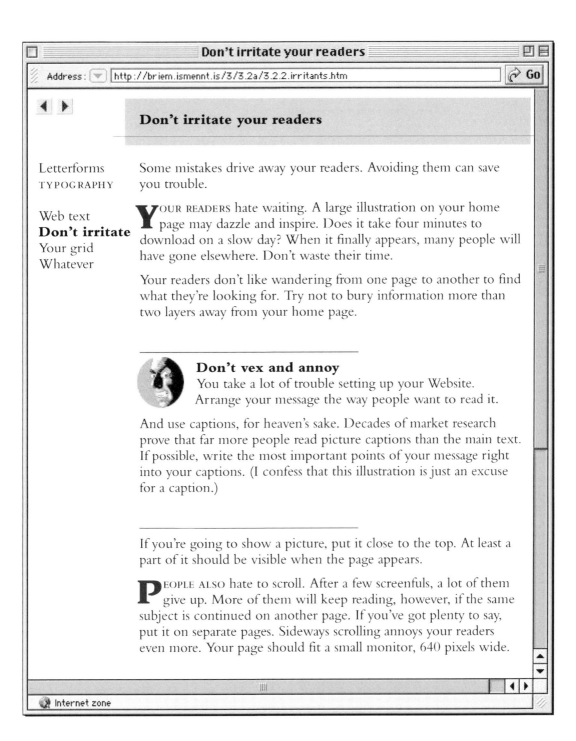

Don't irritate your readers

Letterforms
TYPOGRAPHY

Web text
Don't irritate
Your grid
Whatever

Some mistakes drive away your readers. Avoiding them can save you trouble.

YOUR READERS hate waiting. A large illustration on your home page may dazzle and inspire. Does it take four minutes to download on a slow day? When it finally appears, many people will have gone elsewhere. Don't waste their time.

Your readers don't like wandering from one page to another to find what they're looking for. Try not to bury information more than two layers away from your home page.

Don't vex and annoy
You take a lot of trouble setting up your Website. Arrange your message the way people want to read it.

And use captions, for heaven's sake. Decades of market research prove that far more people read picture captions than the main text. If possible, write the most important points of your message right into your captions. (I confess that this illustration is just an excuse for a caption.)

If you're going to show a picture, put it close to the top. At least a part of it should be visible when the page appears.

PEOPLE ALSO hate to scroll. After a few screenfuls, a lot of them give up. More of them will keep reading, however, if the same subject is continued on another page. If you've got plenty to say, put it on separate pages. Sideways scrolling annoys your readers even more. Your page should fit a small monitor, 640 pixels wide.

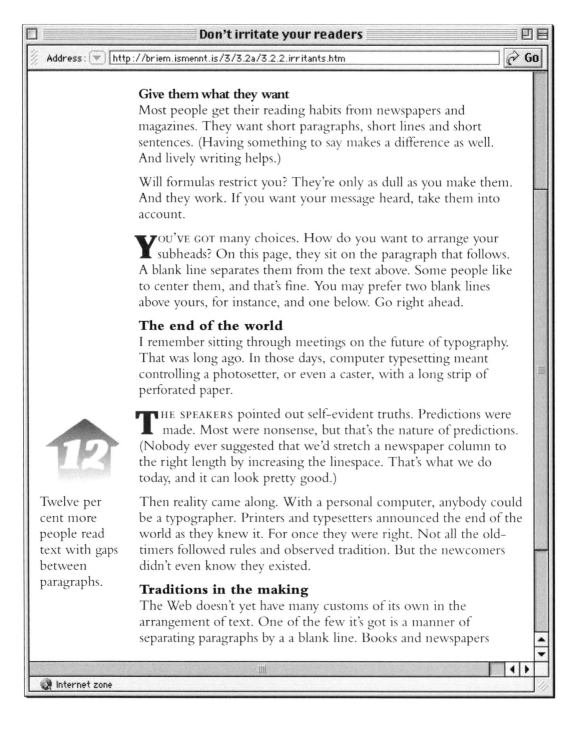

Don't irritate your readers

Address: http://briem.ismennt.is/3/3.2a/3.2.2.irritants.htm | Go

Give them what they want

Most people get their reading habits from newspapers and magazines. They want short paragraphs, short lines and short sentences. (Having something to say makes a difference as well. And lively writing helps.)

Will formulas restrict you? They're only as dull as you make them. And they work. If you want your message heard, take them into account.

YOU'VE GOT many choices. How do you want to arrange your subheads? On this page, they sit on the paragraph that follows. A blank line separates them from the text above. Some people like to center them, and that's fine. You may prefer two blank lines above yours, for instance, and one below. Go right ahead.

The end of the world

I remember sitting through meetings on the future of typography. That was long ago. In those days, computer typesetting meant controlling a photosetter, or even a caster, with a long strip of perforated paper.

THE SPEAKERS pointed out self-evident truths. Predictions were made. Most were nonsense, but that's the nature of predictions. (Nobody ever suggested that we'd stretch a newspaper column to the right length by increasing the linespace. That's what we do today, and it can look pretty good.)

Twelve per cent more people read text with gaps between paragraphs.

Then reality came along. With a personal computer, anybody could be a typographer. Printers and typesetters announced the end of the world as they knew it. For once they were right. Not all the old-timers followed rules and observed tradition. But the newcomers didn't even know they existed.

Traditions in the making

The Web doesn't yet have many customs of its own in the arrangement of text. One of the few it's got is a manner of separating paragraphs by a a blank line. Books and newspapers

Internet zone

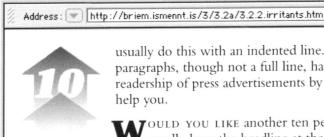

Don't irritate your readers

Address: http://briem.ismennt.is/3/3.2a/3.2.2.irritants.htm   Go

usually do this with an indented line. Extra space between paragraphs, though not a full line, has long been known to increase readership of press advertisements by an average of 12%. This can help you.

WOULD YOU LIKE another ten per cent? Web pages usually have the headline at the top. Illustrations go below it. This is a pity. Advertisements with the illustration above the headline are read by 10% more people than advertisements with the headline at the top. A well-chosen picture makes your readers want to know more.

And an illustration ABOVE the headline can give you ten per cent more readers.

No hurry
At the moment, the Web hardly allows you better typography than a typewriter. Few refinements are possible. No doubt this will change.

When it does, don't rush into anything. Use the tools that everybody has. Meanwhile, use lower case for your headlines. And don't end them with a period. Think of your readers. Keep them happy.

Internet zone

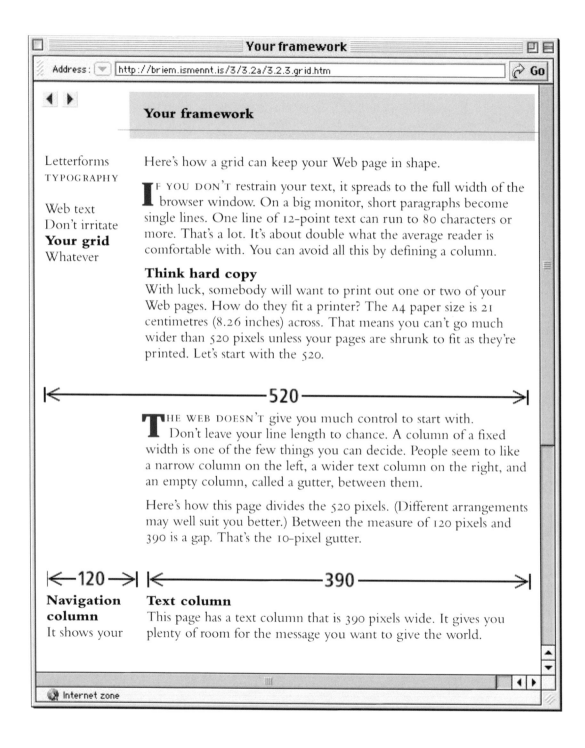

Your framework

Here's how a grid can keep your Web page in shape.

Letterforms
TYPOGRAPHY

Web text
Don't irritate
Your grid
Whatever

IF YOU DON'T restrain your text, it spreads to the full width of the browser window. On a big monitor, short paragraphs become single lines. One line of 12-point text can run to 80 characters or more. That's a lot. It's about double what the average reader is comfortable with. You can avoid all this by defining a column.

Think hard copy
With luck, somebody will want to print out one or two of your Web pages. How do they fit a printer? The A4 paper size is 21 centimetres (8.26 inches) across. That means you can't go much wider than 520 pixels unless your pages are shrunk to fit as they're printed. Let's start with the 520.

|←———————————— 520 ————————————→|

THE WEB DOESN'T give you much control to start with. Don't leave your line length to chance. A column of a fixed width is one of the few things you can decide. People seem to like a narrow column on the left, a wider text column on the right, and an empty column, called a gutter, between them.

Here's how this page divides the 520 pixels. (Different arrangements may well suit you better.) Between the measure of 120 pixels and 390 is a gap. That's the 10-pixel gutter.

|←120→| |←—————————— 390 ——————————→|

Navigation column
It shows your

Text column
This page has a text column that is 390 pixels wide. It gives you plenty of room for the message you want to give the world.

Your framework

Address: http://briem.ismennt.is/3/3.2a/3.2.3.grid.htm   Go

readers where they are on your Website, and where they can go.

It's 120 pixels wide, and divided from the text column by a ten-pixel gutter.

You can also use it for some illustrations and captions.

(There's no need to fill every corner of the screen. White space looks good.) This is where you put your text, most of your illustrations and the captions that go with them.

SEVERAL PARTS make up a Web page. They all have to go somewhere. Your readers like them neatly arranged, and much the same on one page as the next. The pictures should be no broader than the grid. If you need the full 520-pixel width, you can extend the pictures into the navigation column.

The header can have various bits of identification in it, and perhaps your headline as well. It belongs at the top of the page, at least until you start accepting advertisements. (The standard advertising banner is 468 by 60 pixels, and doesn't fit many useful frameworks.)

At the bottom of your page goes the footer, with a date, and perhaps where to reach you. Your readers should also know where you stand on copyright.

Once you've got a layout grid, you can start working on the text itself.

TYPOGRAPHY IS the arrangement of text. People don't like it in one big lump. We divide it into paragraphs and chapters, sentences and sections. Good typography attracts your readers to your message. Bad drives them away.

These are your limits, more or less. They are a proper setting for your ingenuity and invention. Work within them.

Internet zone

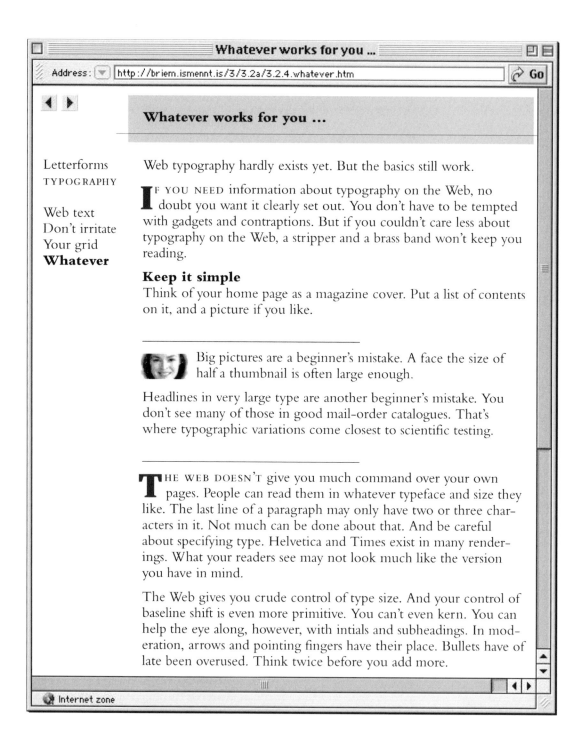

Whatever works for you ...

Address: http://briem.ismennt.is/3/3.2a/3.2.4.whatever.htm

Whatever works for you ...

Letterforms
TYPOGRAPHY

Web text
Don't irritate
Your grid
Whatever

Web typography hardly exists yet. But the basics still work.

IF YOU NEED information about typography on the Web, no doubt you want it clearly set out. You don't have to be tempted with gadgets and contraptions. But if you couldn't care less about typography on the Web, a stripper and a brass band won't keep you reading.

Keep it simple

Think of your home page as a magazine cover. Put a list of contents on it, and a picture if you like.

Big pictures are a beginner's mistake. A face the size of half a thumbnail is often large enough.

Headlines in very large type are another beginner's mistake. You don't see many of those in good mail–order catalogues. That's where typographic variations come closest to scientific testing.

THE WEB DOESN'T give you much command over your own pages. People can read them in whatever typeface and size they like. The last line of a paragraph may only have two or three characters in it. Not much can be done about that. And be careful about specifying type. Helvetica and Times exist in many renderings. What your readers see may not look much like the version you have in mind.

The Web gives you crude control of type size. And your control of baseline shift is even more primitive. You can't even kern. You can help the eye along, however, with intials and subheadings. In moderation, arrows and pointing fingers have their place. Bullets have of late been overused. Think twice before you add more.

Internet zone

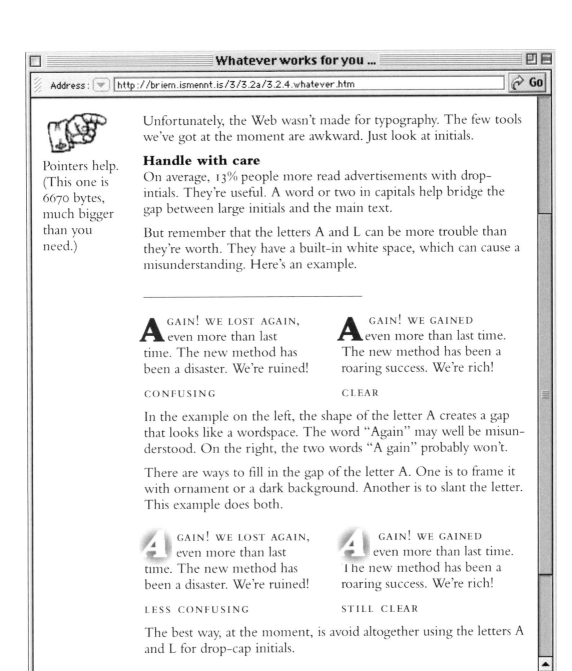

Address: http://briem.ismennt.is/3/3.2a/3.2.4.whatever.htm   Go

Pointers help. (This one is 6670 bytes, much bigger than you need.)

Unfortunately, the Web wasn't made for typography. The few tools we've got at the moment are awkward. Just look at initials.

Handle with care

On average, 13% people more read advertisements with drop-intials. They're useful. A word or two in capitals help bridge the gap between large initials and the main text.

But remember that the letters A and L can be more trouble than they're worth. They have a built-in white space, which can cause a misunderstanding. Here's an example.

AGAIN! WE LOST AGAIN, even more than last time. The new method has been a disaster. We're ruined!

CONFUSING

AGAIN! WE GAINED even more than last time. The new method has been a roaring success. We're rich!

CLEAR

In the example on the left, the shape of the letter A creates a gap that looks like a wordspace. The word "Again" may well be misunderstood. On the right, the two words "A gain" probably won't.

There are ways to fill in the gap of the letter A. One is to frame it with ornament or a dark background. Another is to slant the letter. This example does both.

AGAIN! WE LOST AGAIN, even more than last time. The new method has been a disaster. We're ruined!

LESS CONFUSING

AGAIN! WE GAINED even more than last time. The new method has been a roaring success. We're rich!

STILL CLEAR

The best way, at the moment, is avoid altogether using the letters A and L for drop-cap initials.

Internet zone

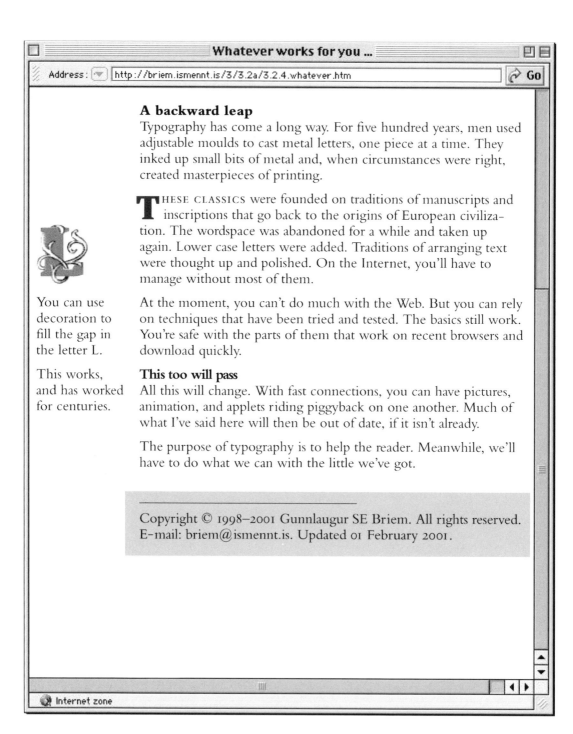

Address: http://briem.ismennt.is/3/3.2a/3.2.4.whatever.htm

Whatever works for you ...

A backward leap

Typography has come a long way. For five hundred years, men used adjustable moulds to cast metal letters, one piece at a time. They inked up small bits of metal and, when circumstances were right, created masterpieces of printing.

THESE CLASSICS were founded on traditions of manuscripts and inscriptions that go back to the origins of European civilization. The wordspace was abandoned for a while and taken up again. Lower case letters were added. Traditions of arranging text were thought up and polished. On the Internet, you'll have to manage without most of them.

You can use decoration to fill the gap in the letter L.

At the moment, you can't do much with the Web. But you can rely on techniques that have been tried and tested. The basics still work. You're safe with the parts of them that work on recent browsers and download quickly.

This works, and has worked for centuries.

This too will pass

All this will change. With fast connections, you can have pictures, animation, and applets riding piggyback on one another. Much of what I've said here will then be out of date, if it isn't already.

The purpose of typography is to help the reader. Meanwhile, we'll have to do what we can with the little we've got.

Copyright © 1998–2001 Gunnlaugur SE Briem. All rights reserved. E-mail: briem@ismennt.is. Updated 01 February 2001.

Internet zone

ARI DAVIDOW

Computer screens are not like paper: typography on the web

To many people, typography is the art of setting beautiful words, using the fonts which best convey the meaning and context of those words. For many years, that was my own approach to the art. I learned to identify at least half a dozen variants of Garamond at 5 paces. I argued and compared settings of Haas Unica vs. Helvetica vs. Frutiger; and of old styles vs. moderns to postmodern faces and grunge, trying to best understand which faces were most appropriate in what circumstances. Finally I focused on actually setting words in the selected typefaces with the best possible spacing, paying close attention to the optical spacing and visual space between letters, between words, and of course, to line length and leading.

These are important issues. To many people, they are typography. It is important to realise, however, that to limit typography to the font, size and leading is to study the details, while missing the forest: the broader issues of communicating print to eye, and of doing so in as economical manner as possible.

What made the invention of the printing press revolutionary was not the fonts. Indeed, I am sure that many contemporaries entirely missed the beauty of those initial books, seeing only that they lacked much of the grace of handwritten manuscript. Instead, the printing press made possible the mass production of books. It opened the door to making more information accessible to more people than ever before in history, more clearly and less expensively. Yet industrialised type is not inherently readable or accessible, it is simply mass-produced. The basis for typography as I understand it is the art of ameliorating that mass production and conveying that more information less expensively, with grace. It was only after years of increasing knowledge that this began to sink in too. (The assumption that I possessed the knowledge was fairly immediate; knowing enough not to be an utter fool took longer.)

Indeed, I was taught to follow specs, to identify typefaces, and to set them well: well-kerned and letterspaced as appropriate; with correctly cut small caps rather than photographic or digital imitations where necessary. I hadn't really paid attention to broader typographic issues except as specified by customers of the type shop wherein I worked.

My epiphany occurred while reading Ferdinand Baudin's *How Typography Works*. This handwritten book on typography first called my attention to the concept of the page. Of course, once I began to think of how letters and words sat upon a page, rather than the beauty of individual letters or words, I came to see pages entirely differently. I was bound to see web pages in terms of access and readability, rather than in tricking a screen not designed for the purpose, into displaying something derived from Simoncini Garamond 12 pt.

For example, having previously missed the critical sections in Ruari McLean's *The Thames and Hudson Manual of Typography*, or Geoffrey Dowding's *Finer Points in the Spacing & Arrangement of Type* (to pick two obvious examples), I now began paying attention to how many words were put on a line. Reading an otherwise well-formed but difficult-to-read book, I would find myself counting the numbers of characters in a series of lines. Sure enough, the move into desktop publishing has opened the field to a plethora of people who confuse visually appealing with "readable." If you consider that 10–12 words, or about 60–65 characters, are as many as the human eye will generally read comfortably in a line of text at standard leading, you will share my discomfort. An astonishing number of books now present difficult-to-muddle-through average line lengths of 80 or 100 characters. The opposite is also true. Books that are easy and comfortable to read, even when the contents are Heidegger or Calculus, seem quite approachable (well, up to a point) when the line length is shorter. There is also a lower limit. When the line length drops below about 40 characters, the length one might see in an average magazine or newspaper column, the average reader becomes impatient.

Poor selection of font, size, line length, and leading became worse when computer word processors began supporting normal type, rather than the fixed-width typewriter imitations with which they began. I found myself calling my students' attention to the fact that no major word processor has been shipped with default line width/type size settings that bore any relationship to visual literacy. Because most early laser printers could be guaranteed to support Helvetica and Times New Roman, people began using the two faces together as though they naturally complement each other. (They don't.) The default typeface in Microsoft Word is Times 10pt, which at the default margins yields an astonishingly opaque 100 characters/line, at a leading (called "line spacing" by much current software) suitable for half that width.

Still, even I was astonished when I began exploring this fascinating new medium, the world wide web. That part of me that has always been interested in making more information available to more people, more quickly, more clearly, and less expensively, is easy to impress with text markup, even the simple markup afforded by the initial HTML specifications.

Yet, when I began to consider issues of "display", I became confused. How does one represent this information most clearly on the computer screen? I found the settings on my "Mosaic" browser for choosing typefaces and sizes. Surprisingly, there appeared to be no controls for page width, or leading. This came as quite a surprise to someone who remembered dedicated typesetting systems that wouldn't let one begin typing until the four "basic" parameters – font, size, page width, leading – were specified. This seemed especially important since text seemed to flow to the width of the window created for the browser, on the reader's computer. That users will attempt to see as much of a web "page" in one view is quite natural, given the affordance, and given the extreme low resolution of standard computer displays. Yet, surely no one would design a text display system in which basic visual literacy could be so violated so unthinkingly?

Since browsers hadn't been designed to allow users to mess with basic typographic controls, I sought them in the HTML specification. I tried earnest study. Then I tried posting in online forums, sure that everyone but me got the joke: "C'mon guys, where are the basic typographic controls?" There were none. And, indeed, when HTML evolved to provide such controls, enough time had passed to realise that such controls were out of context and inappropriate ways of visualizing how to best display information using this new medium.

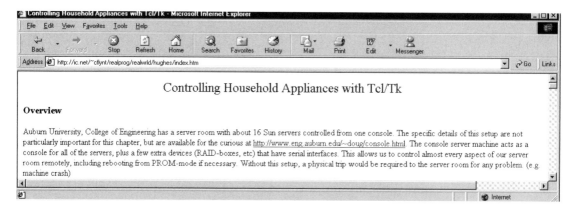

In the meantime, this lack of typographic control did leave many traditional page designers nonplussed. Plausible responses came quickly. Most notably, in 1996, not a year after the web began encroaching upon general public consciousness, David Siegel wrote a book on page design for the web which included, among other things, the idea of placing a plethora of teeny tiny graphics in lines (the "single-pixel gif") such that browsers would increase the space between lines to something that might provide readability.

Those who attempted to follow Siegel's advice soon discovered that it created some enormous problems. The most obvious problem was that anyone viewing such pages without having instructed their web browser to display images (common in that era of slow modems and slow web servers) could no longer read the information. Repurposing the pages and searching them using the new full-text search tools became problematic because of the overflowing cornucopia of irrelevant codes.

The core issue, however, was not leading – any browser manufacturer at any time could have resolved basic viewability by giving users sane defaults or reasonable controls over such parameters. None did, and few users thought to ask. Designers "knew" that typography consisted of being able to specify fonts and sizes and leading, but few apparently had considered the difference between portraying information in a book, or on paper, and portraying that same information on a standard computer screen.

Let's consider. The average "book quality" imagesetter – the poor digital equivalent to the impression and ink flow of cold

This looks quite nice if you are viewing with image display on. Below, see what happens if your browser can't, or isn't, displaying images.

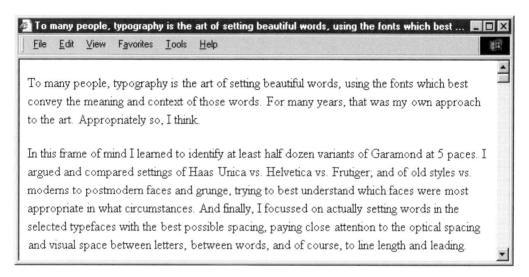

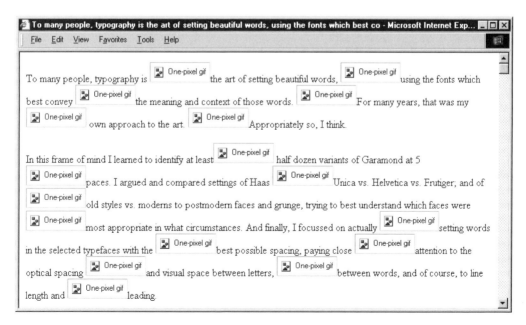

```
<P>To many people, typography is <img src="cl
alt="One-pixel gif">the art of setting beauti
height="18" border="0" alt="One-pixel gif">us
src="clear.gif" width="1" height="18" border=
context of those words. <img src="clear.gif"
alt="One-pixel gif">For many years, that was
height="18" border="0" alt="One-pixel gif"> o
src="clear.gif" width="1" height="18" border=
think.</P>
```

metal – uses about 2500 x 2500 dots per square inch, or over 6 million bits of information. The average computer screen offers less than 100 dots squared (usually 72dpi or 96dpi), which adds up to about 5000 bits of information – less than 1/1000th of the resolution in a common book and many many times less than even the common 600dpi office laserprinter.

One can begin to intuit that good web typography might shape itself differently than good print typography. So when the HTML 4.0 specification incorporated "cascading style sheets" (CSS) in which one could, in fact, specify type size by point (a point, today, being about 1 pixel on a computer screen, or a bit less), and one could specify leading – also in points should one be under the illusion that this was relevant, one could also intuit that this is not dissimilar to having millions of one mark bills in Germany in the 1930s, when it took millions of marks to purchase a potato. The fact that each major web browser understands CSS differently, and evidences different forms of bugginess when interpreting pages coded using CSS, only adds a few extra wheelbarrows of useless currency. (Most notably, CSS styles need to be specified anew in each table cell in Netscape 4. This, at least, is predictable. It is not nearly so debilitating as the fact that the same browser happily interprets separate tables, all specified alike, differently on the same page.)

The quagmire is only deepened when one considers that there are two ways of specifying specifications – what the page designer put on the page, and what the reader specified in his or her personal web controls. Happily, few viewers mess with personal controls, and most, where necessary, can be overridden by the people viewing the pages. Some cannot. The poor viewer who has set his or her web browser to display pages at a large size, so as to overcome problems of distance or vision, is undone by the designer whose wisdom demands specifying specific sizes on the pages. Of course, one need only sit with a Macintosh and a Windows computer side by side to realize that "size" as relates to fonts in a web browser is significantly different between computers.

In addition to the type and size and leading problems, there are other cues available to readers of printed matter that are unavailable to the web. The most important is "foreshadowing." When you pick up a book, you can tell how thick it is, how big the index is, how the chapters are divided, where the illustrations are, and whether or not they are frequent, all at a glance. In two seconds you can follow the page numbers and know how long the item is.

There is no such indicator on the web. There is no easy way to sense how long a web page is, much less what will happen when one follows a hypertext link. It is my belief that this correlates strongly with the desirability of making browser windows as large as possible, the better to see as much of the page as possible, the better to have some idea of what lays on the page without being forced to scroll slowly down, reading each word.

If there is one thing about the web that people universally seem to dislike, it is the unpredictable nature of what constitutes a web page. This is probably one reason why early web behaviour indicated the readers seldom scrolled down a web page. If something was not immediately viewable, they moved on and did not find it. Recent research indicates that readers will scroll down some, but my observation is that people still feel uncomfortable about reading into the unknown, and there are no web tools to help foreshadow anything about the page, except those the web typographer invents.

The key to good typography on the web is thus to eschew traditional type definitions and to focus on what makes a document readable. One must especially address the fact that the web is a very different medium from print, and solve problems that are different from those designing for print. Then, having used what one has learned as a typographer about usability and interface (just as typographers learned from their own writing masters in the

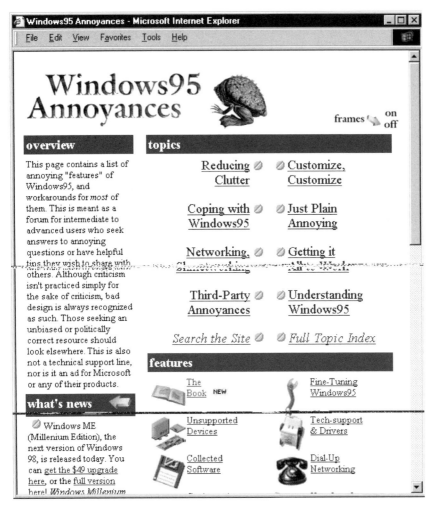

Web 'table of contents'. Note that there is no way to know how much information is there – no foreshadowing, but at least we know what types of information are present.

initial centuries of type) to make the document readable, one reaches back into one's bag of font-related typographic knowledge to add grace.

Basic web typography

First, do no harm. There are a few tricks that one can use that affect basic text parameters. There are also a number of things that one can do that take advantage of finer points of alleged typographic control that will degrade nicely. By "degrade nicely," of course, we mean that browsers that do not understand those commands will

Here is the book based on the website above whose TOC can be viewed, . Not only can we quickly get to more specific locations in the book, but we can see how thick the book is, so we have foreshadowing in two dimensions-specific coordinates, and the overall size and heft of the entire book.

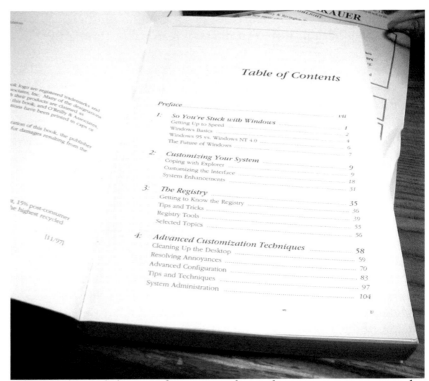

still pass through basic information about document structure and formatting, and where the user has specified default overrides, you don't step on them and make it difficult (or impossible) for the reader to actually read your web page.

Later, we'll also consider things we have learned about making books: printed works that are often read serially, from beginning to end, which also apply quite nicely to the hypertext mishmash layout of websites: dynamic works that are seldom read in contiguous chunks longer than a few paragraphs.

Two basic parameters can be discussed quickly. With regard to font size there is one very important rule. Never specify an absolute size. Never code '<font size="3">1' or '<font size="large">'. Respect the needs of your readers, who, if they have redefined default sizes, have probably done so for good reason. Always use relative font size: '<font size="+1">' or the buggier, but technically valid, '<font size="larger">'.

Next, consider leading. Here's the grim truth. There is no useful way to specify leading in a web environment. You will never have predictable control over line width or font (although there are ways of specifying both in ways that degrade reasonably, through use of CSS).

Life gets more involved when we consider the issue of font. The HTML specification was wisely set up such that one can specify a string of font names, and the first of the fonts specified which is found on the reader's computer, will be used. Should no specified fonts be found, the browser simply defaults to whatever the reader's computer specifies as "default". In addition, there are tools that allow embedding fonts in a webpage, and a new font technology, SVG, which will make this even easier.

Virtually all fonts were designed for print. The visual difference between Sabon and Times New Roman, as seen on a webpage, assuming that the reader has both, in whatever version with whatever viewing technology on his or her computer, is entirely unpredictable. The situation does not necessarily approach guaranteed readability (much less grace) when the fonts are embedded. Where font matters (and it often does, if only in the attempt to display languages which use characters beyond Latin[1], when one can't be assured that the user has such characters available) the use of Adobe's PDF format for a downloadable page is appropriate. Otherwise, where one feels compelled to specify fonts, be careful. If you do not stick to fonts known to exist *only* in versions optimised for the screen display, you can actually create unreadable pages. I have been to many pages specified in a common face such as "Times" which were not readable on the computer on which they were accessed, due to an old and unfortunate version of Times being present.

The only company to pay attention to screen display of fonts, and to make such fonts easily available, is Microsoft[2]. They have a nice set available to individual users, and where they are available on a user's computer, one may be assured that they will be tuned for screen display. In particular, Verdana is a masterpiece of font design, a sans serif at small sizes where each pixel is critical, and a semi-serif in larger sizes. In a less extensive way, and without the cross-platform availability of the Microsoft set, Apple computer has similarly created some notable screen fonts, of which Geneva is probably the best for web display. The true type adaptation of Helvetica, Arial, licensed by both Microsoft and Apple (also available on some/many Unix machines, I believe) is also quite well adapted to the screen. In addition, I sometimes find myself specifying "sans-serif" in an attempt to side-step the general poorer renditions of Times that one sees on most computers, unreadable at small sizes, which is the default display face in most browsers. Thus there is only one font face declaration that I use on almost all web pages where I feel declaring a typeface has merit. There is nothing wrong with declaring other faces that meet the general "all versions to be encountered will have been optimised for screen display" requirement, but, since one can't guarantee their presence on the reader's computer, this almost falls in the category of hidden benefit: an "easter egg", in computer parlance. That basic "will do no harm and occasionally good" font declaration reads: '<font face="verdana,arial,geneva,sans-serif">'.

Line length, or page width, takes us into the trickiest areas of web typography. Not only is there no general code for line length in HTML, even in the CSS section of the later HTML specifications, but the default behaviour is that pages flow to the width of the reader's browser window. The default browser window behaviour on Windows machines (Macintosh defaults seem to be a bit more sensible) is to fill the entire width of the computer screen.

There is only one defence, and it has a touch of the Pyrrhic: Use tables[3]. As I noted earlier, the major browsers differ in their interpretation of instructions as to how to display tables, and may be inconsistent in interpreting the same instructions embedded on the same web page. Nevertheless, simple tables do generally work, and do very much to improve readability by constricting page width. They also provide a simple tool for creating a more complex web page, complete with a navigation area to the left, and a general text area of one or two columns. Exceeding this number of columns risks creating a web page in which readers simply don't discover the rightmost columns. In addition, when designing columns, be aware that those visitors to your website who are vision impaired, and whose interface is audible, not visual, will encounter your table row by row, cell by cell, serially.

The current minimum computer screen display tends to consider of 640 pixels across by 480 pixels down. The more common display size is 800 pixels by 600 pixels, and it is increasingly common to see even more pixels represented on computer screens. The laptop on

which I am editing this article, for instance, is quite comfortable displaying 1024 by 768 pixels.

Since there is no necessary relationship between pixels and any fixed unit of measure (much like "units" in old typesetting systems), one never specifies a table width in inches or centimetres. Rather, one specifies percentages or fixed pixel amounts. In this case, it is usually best to specify a fixed pixel width for the table, and to specify either percentages or fixed widths for the columns. It is important to bear in mind that if you have specified a table to be a fixed width, and that is greater than the available display area on the reader's computer, they will have to scroll horizontally to see part of the table. This will be in addition to the task of scrolling vertically to view most of the length of the page. It is the area of compromise with which I am least comfortable. Yet feedback on my sites in this regard has been positive, leading me to hope that the general numbers I am about to list will meet the needs of enough of a majority to compensate for those few who are discomforted. I have found that when a column exceeds 500 pixels, the line length at common font sizes on common computers, ranges from slightly narrow, to a maximum of readability. I therefore tend to place all text on my web pages into a column that is 480 pixels wide. (The overall table tends to be 600 pixels wide, with 120 pixels devoted to a navigation column on the left-hand side of the page.) Note that if your page includes a graphic that exceeds the width specified for the column, browsers will ignore your specification

Can you see where someone turned on, and then didn't turn off, non-breaking space?

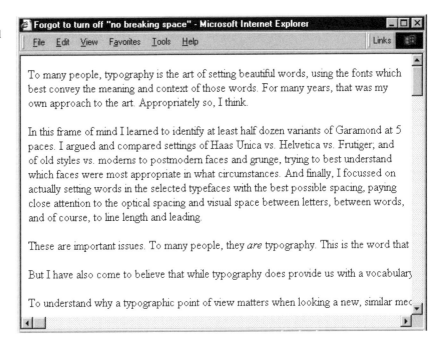

and size the table column to fit the graphic, thus rendering your careful specification moot, and likely to confuse you greatly as you attempt to figure out what has happened. You can achieve a similarly awful effect by using the <pre> tag, which tells the browser to treat your text endings literally – and to expand the column to fit the lines as they come out on display, or by turning on the <nobr>4 command and forgetting to terminate it with </nobr>. Obviously, you would be in similar visual hot water even if you weren't using tables. Be careful!

Advanced Web Typography
To be stuck with only these basic tools and options must surely strike most typographers as bleak. Awaiting higher resolution monitors and better ways of displaying information well on a computer screen is fine for the theorists, but one prime directive confronting all typographers is the need to make the medium transparent to the text with the means at hand.

The first easy way to add typographic variety to web pages is to create text-as-graphic. The well-designed drop-cap, inserted as a text image, aligned left, will add grace points to any manuscript.

Similarly, the careful use of headlines set in appropriate typefaces (simpler lines will work better than complex ones, at small sizes, of course) provides a nice way to break up text, albeit at the expense of causing the page to take longer to download (only slightly longer, if one uses care) and the danger of making the headline less searchable or visible. This latter is partially alleviated by the use of anchored names and "alt" tags. Creating an appropriate table of contents at the top of a page, using text links to the subsections below, ensures that the heads are indexed. Thus:

```
<p><a name="advanced"></a><img
src="images/advanced.gif" height="37" width="243"
vspace="4" alt="Advanced Web Typography"></p>
   <p>To be stuck with.....
```

Note that in the above example, I also use the HTML "vspace" command to ensure that some extra space is left surrounding the head. Unfortunately, this does not provide me with the means to ensure that traditional extra dollop of space above the head, so that it is visually associated with what follows. That is resolved either by building some extra white space into the top of the headline graphic, or, more succinctly, by simply prefixing the paragraph with a hard return, followed by a non-breaking space (the latter necessary so that the web browser logic will see a line with something on it, rather than an empty line to be ignored, code-wise). Thus:

```
<p><a name="advanced"></a> <br><img....
```

Note also that I have used the paragraph as a container, with both a beginning and an end code. This coding style has the technical advantage of being compatible with XHTML and XML, and the even better typographic advantage of making it very clear what part of your text is part of the paragraph, to be differentiated, top and bottom, in whatever means the browser differentiates between paragraphs[5].

I especially love this system in which one foreshadows what is present on a page by the placement of the heads in a small table of contents at the top of the page, with links to each subhead. Next to each subhead, in the navigation column, one can also place links back to the top of the page. Where this is inconvenient, one can place the text link at the top in a smaller font size, differentiated perhaps by square brackets, at the end of each section [to top of

Although these fonts look relatively similar in their GIF representations, this particular older Macintosh delights in presenting wildly unrelated, and not-particularly readable variants on the themes. The solution does not lie in trying to replace each font with more recent variants; it lies, for the most part, in not treating HTML as one would an PDF. Leave font specification to the user, whenever and wherever possible, lest you make it impossible for your site viewers to actually read your site!

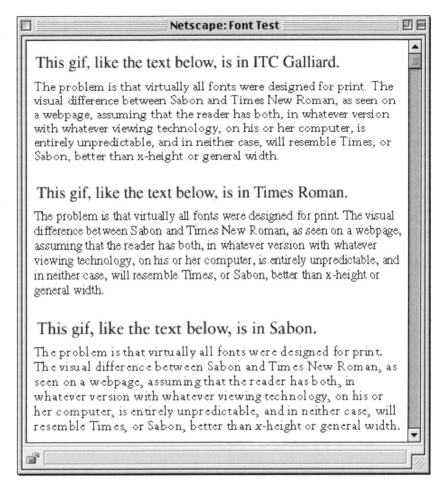

page]. This provides the reader with the best of both worlds: he or she can quickly explore the page, just as he or she can quickly move to those parts of the page that are most interesting. (If your page is a short story, other navigation criteria may apply; if your page is a novel, there are additional issues, of course.)

In addition to the miniature table of contents at the top of a web page indicating what is present on the page, a common good use of the left-hand navigation bar is to place a series of pages in context, so that the reader can quickly jump between pages, taking good advantage of the web's hypertext linking back and forth. Taken together, these make the web a medium in which a variety of non-serial uses of print, from finding technical information to viewing an art exhibit, can be seriously enhanced in ways that have never worked well for print.

Although use of graphics in place of text for heads and subheads can be used to add color and typographic finery to a page, care must be used in substituting graphics for text. As I wrote earlier, this does slow the display of the page up, usually slightly, and does make the page slightly more complex to maintain (another graphic to keep track of, and one which must be recreated whenever editing changes the subhead). Recent studies have clearly shown that web page readers understand and use links that consist of text to a far greater degree than the same link anchored to a graphic. So, while use of graphics as headlines carries a minimal penalty, substitution of image maps and icons for text links is often a bad idea. And, obviously, one would never want to force the user to an image map for navigation, if only because not all readers can see graphics.

In addition to these tricks, one can add text as needed to graphic elements by use of the ECMAscript (née "JavaScript") "onMouseOver" commands. Thus:

<a href="#ramble" onMouseOver="self.status='This will take you down the page to a rambling piece about typography and the web and what I do for a living.';return true;">what I do for a living</a>

will cause the reader to get some information about the link prior to clicking and experimenting. In this particular case, the information appears on the status bar at the bottom of the screen. A better system would be similar to what occurs using the "alt" tag on an image – a floating text box next to where the reader is currently reading.

Cascading Style Sheets

I have separated out my discussion of Cascading Style Sheets (CSS) from the rest of the discussion of advanced typography because CSS is wonderful, easy to use, well-documented, and only occasionally implemented partially as specified. This means that you can easily use CSS to redefine your levels of head, and other elements, to typographic perfection, but that many browsers will misinterpret CSS, or ignore it. In particular, Netscape Navigator through current non-beta releases, needs the CSS to be restated in each and every table cell, either by use of the <span> tag, or by use of a redefined paragraph tag, or otherwise. This is tedious, but can be accomplished with some reasonable speed when using visual HTML editors such as DreamWeaver or GoLive, without paying any particular attention to the HTML, or learning the finer features thereof.

When you use CSS by redefining elements (or by defining alternate variants, using the "class" commands) you also specify your set up for the most graceful degradation possible. Browsers that correctly understand your CSS codes will work perfectly. Those that do not, have only to use the proper HTML that you coded, and will still display the elements properly differentiated, as defined by the browser defaults. This may not be graceful, but at least you stay out of the way of users for whom those codes had no meaning. It's a win/win situation.

As I mentioned in an earlier footnote, the one thing you most want to avoid is to substitute CSS or raw font redefinition codes

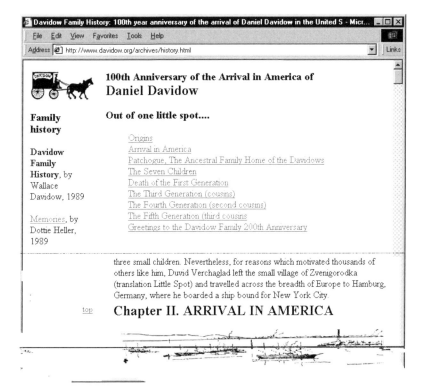

for the actual HTML commands. You absolutely want browsers to know what is a head, and at what level; what is a paragraph, and so on. Attempts to sidestep these built-in document definition helpers will result in visual jumble similar to what happens when a word processed document, in which the typist used the space bar to achieve perfect horizontal placement, is suddenly viewed at another size, or in a different typeface, or simply on a different machine which uses different default page parameters or font metrics. Don't go there. If you are there, consult your HTML guides and reconsider!

Ultimate Typography on the Web

Given the constraints created by today's web browsers, and by HTML itself, typography, as it is understood to relate to fonts, might seem irrelevant to the web. As I hope I have shown, this is not true, although the issues and their solutions are different than those used for print. Sometimes, however, precise typography matters. This may be as simple as the need to take a newsletter, with known page and column breaks, and make it universally viewable. It may include the use of custom symbols (although these can also be accommodated by small graphics on the web page), or different alphabets. It may be a case where a complex form or complex table needs to be presented clearly and within the physical constraints of a typical browser window.

Adobe has solved this problem by creating the "portable document format" (PDF). Viewers for PDFs, the Adobe Acrobat Reader, are available free from Adobe's website[6]. Adobe Acrobat is relatively inexpensive (appr. $300) and current versions allow one to print directly from document to PDF, as well as to embed a host of links within the document or to sites on the web external to the document. I use the format frequently for multilingual material, or for broadsides that incorporate type and graphic in a specific layout. Mastering PDF has the additional advantage of being significantly simpler than HTML!

Summary

When discussing typography on the web, one must hark back to the origins of Western typography to consider issues of mass production and easier, more affordable access to more information.

Many issues of font and leading have no relevant analogues, and the attempt to treat the web as print is to attempt the irrelevant and impossible, while simultaneously ignoring the wonderful new tools. These new tools include hypertext linking, and the ability to display parts of text according to what you say they are, dependent on the reader's needs – visible or audible or otherwise.

Issues less relevant or noted in the print world, but absolutely critical to the web, focus very much on navigation and foreshadowing. People are used to judging what they are about to read by what they know about it. On the web, there is no physical item to heft, no way to quickly fan the pages. In a web page which demonstrates excellent typography, and produces the same excellence of interface, and visual grace equivalent to that of a good book, one can do things which facilitate finding information. This also lets the reader construct his or her own narrative in ways that print designers cannot even conceive. The media are different. The challenges are similar, and what one has learned as a print typographer will stand one in good stead, provided that one is looking at the forest, rather than cataloguing only the trees.

Footnotes

1   You will note that all attributes of HTML commands in this article are surrounded by double quote marks. The HTML specification is much more lenient. Unless an attribute contains spaces, as might happen in a multi-word "alt" tag on an image, these quotes are unnecessary. However, XML and XHTML, the emerging new generation of web markup languages do unambiguously require quote marks around all attributes.

2   insert URL here

3   You can also use frames to achieve this purpose. Use of frames, however, generally renders a site difficult to navigate and confusing to the user, so that one would not consider their discussion consistent with "web typography." See, for instance, Jakob Nielsen's recent book on Web interface.

4   This command is deprecated in HTML 4.0, which means that one should not expect future browser versions to support it. It has probably occurred to the standards people that it is far less dangerous to put non-breaking spaces where desired, one by one, using the   entity.

5   Contemporary browsers favour the technical documentation style in which extra space is left to vertically differentiate paragraphs, rather than an indent at the beginning of a paragraph. This style is very useful in technical documentation where indentation often carries additional meaning, but is unfortunate in a text context, where a paragraph indent would be preferred, could it be defined. When HTML

allows you to redefine the paragraph, that would be a useful and graceful thing to do. Under no circumstances, as I discuss shortly, should one attempt to force specific visual effect, however, by sidestepping HTML codes and attempting to build display by use of, say, <br> codes between paragraphs, which then begin with several non-breaking spaces. That would be pandering to an unfortunate typewriter convention, effectively making the semantic meaning of the paragraph invisible to search engines and other tools which work with the text. Although typographers are trained to focus on visual display, in this medium, semantic definition, use of appropriate HTML tags is significant, and not to be short-changed by a visual display that will work only on some browsers and leave others entirely without means to interpret the implied, missing text elements.

6   http://www.adobe.com/

Bibliography

Baudin, Fernand. 1988. *How Typography Works (and why it is important)*. (London: Lund Humphries Publishers Ltd.)

Dowding, Geoffrey. 1995. *Finer Points in the spacing & arrangement of TYPE*. (Vancouver: Hartley & Marks Publishers, Inc. First published by Wace & Company Ltd., London, 1954.)

McLean, Ruari. 1980. *The Thames and Hudson Manual of Typography*. (London: Thames and Hudson Ltd.)

Nielsen, Jakob. 1999. *Designing Web Usability: The Practice of Simplicity*. (Indianapolis: New Riders Publishing)

PART 2

NON-LATIN TYPOGRAPHY

Non-Latin typesetting in the digital age

FIONA ROSS TYPOGRAPHIC CONSULTANT IN NON-LATIN SCRIPTS

fiona@rosstype.demon.co.uk

'Digital technology coupled with innovative software ushered in an era of enormous potential for non-Latin typefaces.'

English, Japanese and the computer

EIICHI KONO GRAPHIC DESIGNER kono@dial.pipex.com

'The computer is getting more and more powerful. Wonderful things have happened to our complicated writing system in the last five years. Japanese is now the second most used language on the Internet after English.'

FIONA ROSS

Non-Latin typesetting in the digital age

Non-Latin typesetting encompasses an enormous variety of scripts which are employed by a large percentage of the world's population. Reproducing these often complex writing systems in print, usually by processes originally designed for Latin types, has always presented a challenge; and the legacy of earlier typefounding practices is evident in today's fonts.

The history of printing with non-Latin characters can be dated back to an eighth-century, block-printed incantation found in Korea.[1] There is evidence of a smith and alchemist, Bi Sheng, producing movable clay types in China in 1045 AD. The succeeding centuries have seen the reproduction of different writing systems in print by means of wood, porcelain, stone, metal, and more recently, film. But current digital font technology and typesetting software probably affords the greatest opportunity to faithfully render non-Latin scripts in readable, high-quality typeforms.

Requirements for non-Latin composition differ radically from country to country, and may also vary from region to region. However, the most common feature found in the majority of these scripts – and one of the most technically challenging – has been the large size of the character repertoires, causing problems of font storage (and high production costs). Few languages need the vast array of Chinese *Kanji* characters, but most scripts require in excess of 256 sorts, even those with relatively modest basic 'alphabets'. For instance, an inherent feature of both written and typeset Arabic is that the shape of a letter can vary depending on its position within a word; in consequence many characters can have up to four forms (figure 1). Other scripts require extensive character sets to represent phonemic combinations.

Typefounding records of the nineteenth century reveal a drive, occasioned by economic necessity, to reduce the number of

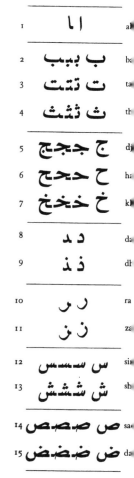

Figure 1. Part of an Arabic letterform chart by Linotype and Machinery Limited, c.1950s.

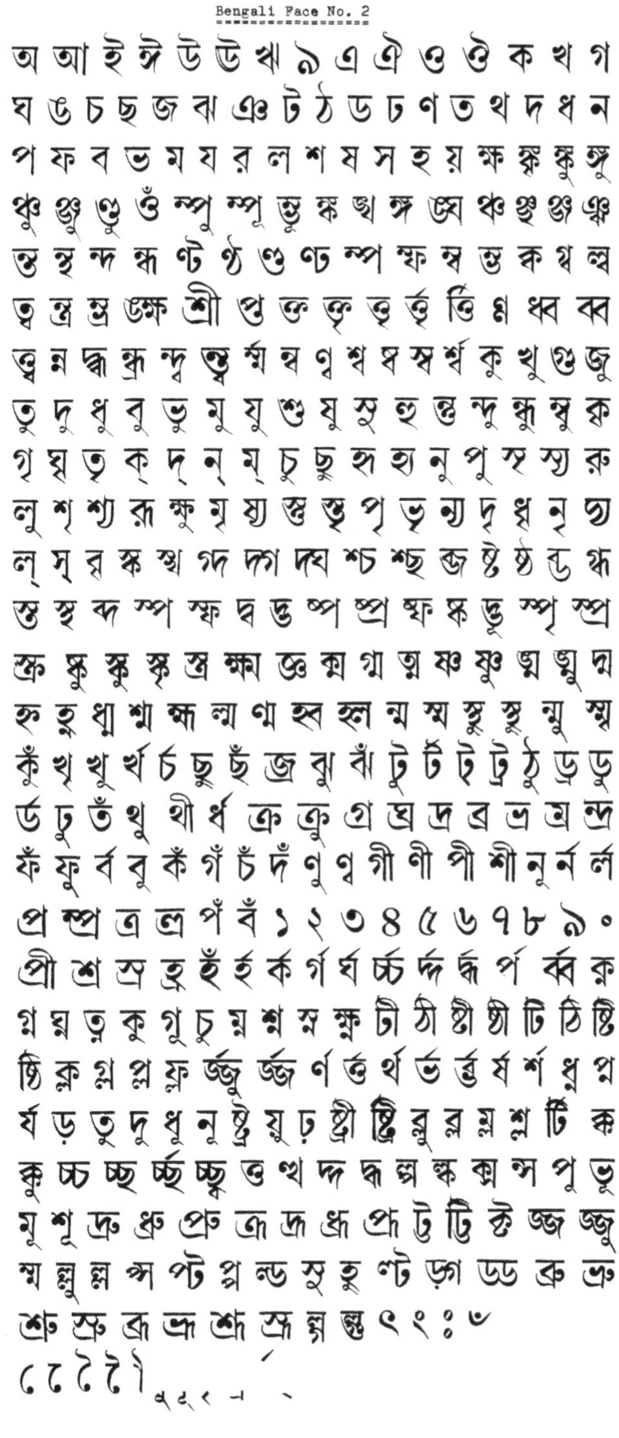

Bengali Face No. 2

Figure 2. Bengali foundry font from Calcutta (reduced, right).

লাইনোটাইপ বাঙ্গলা নং ২-এর সাথে বোল্ড ফেস্ নং ২

◆◆◆

LIST OF CHARACTERS IN THE FOUNT

লাইনোটাইপ বাংলা লাইট এবং বোল্ড

'ফণ্ট'-ভুক্ত অক্ষরচিহ্ন

12 point (12△472)   ১২ পয়েণ্ট

In Magazine   ম্যাগাজিনে

া ি নে ্য ী অ ত র ব ল গ ম ক হ য ছ শ য স দ প এ ্ জ ' ণ ই ট
া ি নে ্য ী অ ত র ব ল গ ম ক হ য ছ শ য স দ প এ ্ জ ' ণ ই ট
প্র — , ঃ ? র্ ৃ - ₹ ও ঃ খ থ থ ধ ষ ভ উ ₨ গ ্ ং ক্ষ ক্
প্র — , ঃ ? র্ ৃ - ₹ ও ঃ খ থ থ ধ ষ ভ উ ₨ গ ্ ং ক্ষ ক্
ড় র ঘ ড ঐ ৎ জ্ঞ ফ তু চ জ ত্ক কু শ্রী দ্ ঝ কৃ ভু ভ ঠ ভূ ্ে আ ছ ব
ড় র ঘ ড ঐ ৎ জ্ঞ ফ তু চ জ ত্ক কু শ্রী দ্ ঝ কৃ ভু ভ ঠ ভূ ্ে আ ছ র
ট্র ী ট্ ১ ২ ৩ ৪ ৫ ৬ ৭ ৮ ৯ ০ ৺ । ' ং ; ' চূ ঢ (ী ' কৃ ঃ শ্র
ট্র ী ট্ ত্ত ত্ত ম্ল ক্ষ ড্ড ড্র ল্ল ত্ন ন্ন কৃ ৺ । ' ং ; ' চূ ্র ঢ (ী ' কৃ ঃ শ্র
) ঝ ঙ চ্ছ ব ড্র ম্ল ম্ম হ্ন
) ঝ ঙ চ্ছ ব ড্র ম্ল ম্ম হ্ন

Pie Characters   ম্যাগাজিনের বাহিরে

১ ২ ৩ ৪ ৫ ৬ ৭ ৮ ৯ ০ ঈ উ ঋ ঔ ঙ এ্ঞ ড় দ্ব দ্ধ ক্ক ক্র ক্ট ক্ক ক্ক ক
ত্ ত্ত ম্র ষ্ফ ড্ড ড্র ল্ল ত্ন ন্ন কৃ ঈ উ ঋ ঔ ঙ এ্ঞ ড় দ্ব দ্ধ ক্ক ক্র ক্ট ক্ক ক্ক ক
ফ্র ফ্র স্র হ হ হ্ন * ধ থ থ্ব ঘ্ন ষ্ণ ঁ ম্ন · ত্র র্ ঃ ৃ ৗ [ ] ঃ জ্র কৃ কৃ
ফ্র ফ্র স্র হ হ হ্ন * ধ থ থ্ব ঘ্ন ষ্ণ ঁ ম্ন · ত্র র্ ঃ ৃ ৗ [ ] ঃ জ্র কৃ কৃ
প্র প্র ষ্ঠ ২ ওঁ জ্ঞ ক শ্র ক্ক ক্তু ত্তু ক্ত দ্ধ ধ ণ্ঠ ত্র ত্র ষ্ঠ ম্র ন্ত শ্র প্র ক
প্র প্র ষ্ঠ ২ ওঁ জ্ঞ ক শ্র ক্ক ক্তু ত্তু ক্ত দ্ধ ধ ণ্ঠ ত্র ত্র ষ্ঠ ম্র ন্ত শ্র প্র ক
+ − × ÷ = ত্র ত্র ড্র ড্র ট্র ট্র দ্র ঞ্চ দ্র ড্র ড্র ট্র ট্র ড ক্ষ " শ্র ্র ্র
+ − × ÷ = ত্র ত্র ড্র ড্র ট্র ট্র দ্র ঞ্চ দ্র ড্র ড্র ট্র ট্র ড ক্ষ " শ্র ্র ্র
কৃ কৃ ফ্র ¶ † ‡ র্ী ড্র ড্র ্র দ্র দ্র দ্র দ্র § শ্র ⁄ ⁄ ‖ ‖ ৲ ৹ ৴
কৃ কৃ ফ্র ¶ † ‡ র্ী ড্র ড্র ্র দ্র দ্র দ্র দ্র § শ্র ⁄ ⁄ ‖ ‖ ৲ ৹ ৴

Figure 3. Hot-metal Linotype Bengali No. 2 with Bold Face No 2 (left).

Figure 4. Hot-metal Linotype Yakout 'simplified' font synopsis.

CHARACTERS IN THE FOUNT · KEYBOARD 382C

528	الـ	019	خ	036	غ	055	ﻉ	430	٣
01	ا	020	د	037	ذ	056	ﻉ	431	٤
01A	ا	021	ذ	038	غ	144	ة	432	٥
066	أ	022	ر	039	ف	071	ة	433	٦
02	بـ	023	ز	040	ف	057	و	434	٧
03	ـبـ	024	س	041	ق	063	ؤ	435	٨
04	ت	061	ـ	042	ق	058	ي	436	٩
05	ت	025	س	043	ك	058A	ى	437	٠
06	ث	026	ش	044	ﻚ	167A	ي	445	!
07	ث	027	ص	045	ل	167	ى	446	؟
08	ج	028	ض	076	ل	059	ﺋ	454	:
09A	ﺟ	029	ط	047	م	062	ﺉ	455	'
011	ﺠ	030	ظ	048	ﻣ	132	لا	456	)
012	ح	031	ع	051	ن	133	لا	457	(
013A	ﺣ	032	ـع	052	ن	5	—	458	»
015	ﺤ	033	ﻣ	053	ه	443	ء	459	«
016	خ	034	ع	054	ﻪ	428	١	EN SPACE	
017A	ﺨ	035	غ			429	٢	EM SPACE	

CHARACTERS IN THE SIDE CASE

068	أ	075	لله	558	لا	605	×	539	٢/٣
070	آ	62	ﺮ	450	★	606	=	540	١/٢
159A	ي	176	ﺮ	453	·	607	—	750	●
159	ى	204	ين	561	,	608	÷	751	★
072	لى	329	ﺋ	449	؛	630	/	Thin Space	
073	لى	559	لا	570	ﭒ	532	١/٤		
074	في	557	لا	580	٪	535	٣/٤		
074A	ﻗ	560	لا	604	+	537	١/٣		

characters in scripts by using common components to generate letterforms. The often unsatisfactory results were subseqently compounded in the first half of the twentieth century by the era of hot-metal composition in the production of line-caster fonts for composing electoral rolls and vernacular newspapers.

Comparisons of the sizes of early foundry fonts to those of the mid-twentieth century show the discontinued use of hundreds of typeforms in many Indian scripts, even in book production (figures 2 and 3). The small character sets of 96 sorts (plus pi characters), combined with the linecaster's inability to kern and position 'accents' correctly, engendered possibly the greatest divergence between the written hand and the printed character in non-Latin scripts: in printed Devanagari vertically-stacked conjuncts were almost eradicated; the Malayalam script saw the introduction of vowel-sign characters divorced from their host consonants; and readers complained that Bengali letterforms had been 'mutilated'.

Arabic fonts were also 'simplified' for newspaper setting: Linotype and Machinery Limited's Yakout typeface used a reduced number of contextual forms (figure 4) so that "alphabet characters" decreased "from 104 to 56"; it dispensed with diacriticals – apart from a few "necessary 'pointed' characters"[2]; and it omitted the majority of Arabic ligatures.[3]

The lower production costs of linear fonts combined with the use of rotary printing benefited the wider dissemination of printed vernacular material. However, in the Indian subcontinent the impaired readability of the resultant printed matter did not lead to the desired increases in literacy, since it created two types of readership. There were readers who were conversant with all the lettershapes found in manuscript (figure 5) and with the typeforms employed by traditional typefoundries, and readers whose reading material was confined to newspapers and who were unable to read traditional typeforms – or even the written script. Thus linear composition did little to further the cause in India of replacing English as the lingua franca with the official national language, Hindi (figure 6).

Typesetting constraints were ameliorated by the introduction of photocomposition, although its full benefits did not affect non-Latin composition until the 1970s. At last, with the possibility of overlapping joins, the white gap visible between characters of a

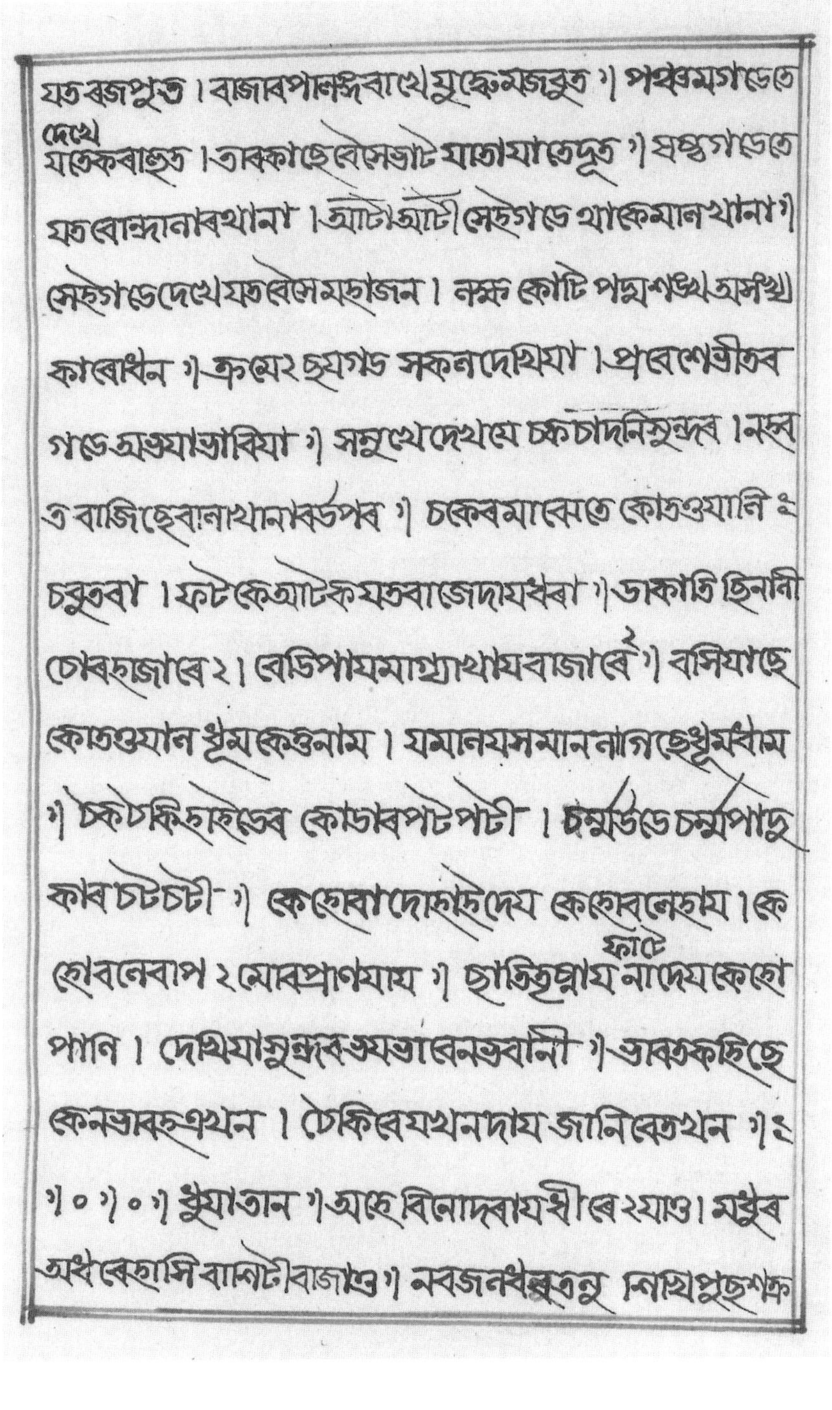

Figure 5. Eighteenth century Bengali manuscript (decorative hand). From BL MS Add 5593 – Vidyasundara. British Library.

लाइनोटाइप दॅवनागरी लाइट और बोल्ड

14 point (14△224) १४-पाइंट

लाइनोटाइप के मुद्रण-साधन जग-प्रख्यात हैं । प्रायः ८५० से अधिक
भाषाओं अेवं बोलियों का काम इसके की-बोर्ड पर किया जा सकता हैं । ये
तथ्य इस बात के प्रमाण हैं कि ब्रिटिश और अमेरिकन लाइनोटाइप संस्थाओं
ने स्लग कंपोजिशन विधि (जिसके दूसरी विधियों की तुलना में कई लाभ
हैं) का अनेक जातियों और अनेक भाषाओं के लोगों को लाभ पहुंचाया हैं ।
इस पद्धति में अन्य पद्धतियों के गुणों के अतिरिक्त स्वयं अपने बहुत से गुण
हैं जो इसकी प्रशस्ति का कारण हैं । प्रत्येक देश के बुद्धिमान विशेषज्ञों के
विशिष्ट प्रयत्नों के परिणाम-स्वरूप आज यह पद्धति सारे विश्व में समाचार-
पत्रों, पुस्तकों अेवं अन्य वस्तुओं की छपाई के लिये प्रचलित हैं । वास्तव में
लाइनोटाइप का आविष्कार रोमन अक्षरों के लिये ही किया गया था, परंतु आज
दॅवनागरी जैसी क्लिष्ट लिपियों का काम भी इस मशीन पर आसानी से किया
जा सकता हैं । यही नहीं, यह मशीन इन सभी विविध अक्षरों के लिये समान

Figure 6. Hot-metal Linotype Devanagari Light with Bold.

Figure 7. Lotus type specimen, a popular film font now translated into digital type (right).

connecting script could be eradicated. More importantly, software
began to be introduced which could select contextual forms. This
technology was particularly tested by scripts of different reading
directions for which special software was devised. Software also
handled the positioning of vowel signs by double exposure, and
implemented the logic needed for automatic justification. Some
very fine Arabic fonts were designed during this period that remain
popular today (figure 7).

However, the popularity of foundry types or the use of
calligraphers and lithography for high quality book-setting
continued in many countries due to economic constraints; the
limited selection of suitable non-Latin film fonts; and the
limitations filmsetting still imposed on some scripts, notably
Bengali. In the case of Urdu, Nasta'liq calligraphers remained
unrivalled.[4] Moreover, in countries where the oral tradition was
strong and the manual copying of sacred texts constituted a
meritorious act, the use of printing types was still regarded as
undesirable.

Digital technology coupled with innovative software ushered in

Figure 8. Urdu film advertisement from Inquilab Daily (Bombay, 1993).

لوتس

وَضَعَتْ لَيْنوتَيْبْ ـ هِلْ مَقَايِيسَ رفيعَةً لِتَصْميم وَإِنْتاج خُطوطٍ عَرَبِيَّةٍ عالِيَةِ الجَوْدَةِ. وَتَحْتَوي مَكْتَبُها الْيَوْمَ عَلى خُطوطٍ «بوسْتْ سْكْرِيثْ» المَعْروفَةِ باسْمِ «النَّوع ١» وَالشَّامِلَةِ عَلى كُلِّ المَعْلوماتِ اللازِمَةِ لإخْراج نَوعِيَّةٍ مُمْتازَةٍ مِنْ

وَضَعَتْ لَيْنوتَيْبْ ـ هِلْ مَقَايِيسَ رفيعَةً لِتَصْميم وَإِنْتاج خُطوطٍ عَرَبِيَّةٍ عالِيَةِ الجَوْدَةِ. وَتَحْتَوي مَكْتَبُها الْيَوْمَ عَلى خُطوطٍ «بوسْتْ سْكْرِيثْ» المَعْروفَةِ باسْمِ «النَّوع ١» وَالشَّامِلَةِ عَلى كُلِّ المَعْلومات

وَضَعَتْ لَيْنوتَيْبْ ـ هِلْ مَقَايِيسَ رفيعَةً لِتَصْميم وَإِنْتاج خُطوطٍ عَرَبِيَّةٍ عالِيَةِ الجَوْدَةِ. وَتَحْتَوي مَكْتَبُها الْيَوْمَ عَلى خُطوطٍ «بوسْتْ سْكْرِيثْ» المَعْروفَةِ باسْمِ «النَّوع ١»

وَضَعَتْ لَيْنوتَيْبْ ـ هِلْ مَقَايِيسَ رفيعَةً لِتَصْميم وَإِنْتاج خُطوطٍ عَرَبِيَّةٍ عالِيَةِ الجَوْدَةِ. وَتَحْتَوي مَكْتَبُها الْيَوْمَ عَلى خُطوطٍ «بوسْتْ سْكْرِيثْ» المَعْروفَةِ باسْمِ «النَّوع ١» وَالشَّامِلَةِ عَلى كُلِّ المَعْلوماتِ اللازِمَةِ لإخْراج نَوعِيَّةٍ مُمْتازَةٍ مِنْ

وَضَعَتْ لَيْنوتَيْبْ ـ هِلْ مَقَايِيسَ رفيعَةً لِتَصْميم وَإِنْتاج خُطوطٍ عَرَبِيَّةٍ عالِيَةِ الجَوْدَةِ. وَتَحْتَوي مَكْتَبُها الْيَوْمَ عَلى خُطوطٍ «بوسْتْ سْكْرِيثْ» المَعْروفَةِ باسْمِ «النَّوع ١» وَالشَّامِلَةِ عَلى كُلِّ المَعْلوماتِ

وَضَعَتْ لَيْنوتَيْبْ ـ هِلْ مَقَايِيسَ رفيعَةً لِتَصْميم وَإِنْتاج خُطوطٍ عَرَبِيَّةٍ عالِيَةِ الجَوْدَةِ. وَتَحْتَوي مَكْتَبُها الْيَوْمَ عَلى خُطوطٍ «بوسْتْ سْكْرِيثْ» المَعْروفَةِ باسْمِ «النَّوع

an era of enormous potential for non-Latin typesetting. The *phonetic keyboard,* which was first invented for Indian scripts by Linotype-Paul Limited in 1978,[5] heralded the demise of the large keyboard introduced for non-Latin photocomposition. In particular it revolutionised keyboarding procedures for Indian scripts. Based on the Indian phonological writing system, the operator could now touch-type phonetically from a standard keyboard and gain access not only to contextual forms (as achieved by filmsetting), but a full repertoire of conjuncts (figure 9), ligatures, alternative forms, as well as potentially thousands of specified character combinations. The disentangling of the *phonetic keyboard* from the output device gave designers and font manufacturers hitherto inconceivable flexibility in determining font contents and layouts (even two typestyles of the same typeface did not need to share the same font synopsis). The *phonetic keyboard* has been adopted in a variety of guises throughout the Indian subcontinent.

The possibility afforded by digital technology to merge font units no longer restricted the size of character repertoires; wide characters, which abound in some scripts like Tamil and Sinhala (figures 10 and 11), no longer demanded an overall reduction in body heights; furthermore, subscripts and superscripts could be positioned far more accurately than in filmsetting (figure 12). Even with the introduction of the PostScript page description language in the 1980s,[6] which standardised font formats and composing software for device-independent output, sophisticated non-Latin software was needed to provide complex justification logic (as required in Thai composition) and simultaneously handle scripts of different reading directions and variable baselines. Thus readable, rather than merely legible, type

ক + ক = ক্ক   ঙ + ঘ = ঙ্ঘ   ণ + ঠ = ণ্ঠ

ক + ট = ক্ট   ঙ + ম = ঙ্ম   ণ + ড = ণ্ড

ক + ত = ক্ত   চ + চ = চ্চ   ণ + ড + ৱ = ণ্ড্ৰ

ক + ন = ক্ন   চ + ছ = চ্ছ   ণ + ণ = ণ্ণ

ক + ব = ক্ব   চ + ছ + ব = চ্ছ্ব   ণ + ঢ = ণ্ঢ

ক + ম = ক্ম   চ + এঙ = চ্ঞ   ণ + ব = ণ্ব

ক + ৱ = ক্ৰ   চ + ছ + ৱ = চ্ছ্ৰ   ণ + ম = ণ্ম

ক + ল = ক্ল   ছ + ৱ = ছ্ৰ   ত + ত = ত্ত

ক + স = ক্স   জ + জ = জ্জ   ত + ত + ব = ত্ত্ব

ক + ষ = ক্ষ   জ + জ + ব = জ্জ্ব   ত + থ = ত্থ

খ + ৱ = খ্ৰ   জ + ঝ = জ্ঝ   ত + ন = ত্ন

গ + গ = গ্গ   জ + এঙ = জ্ঞ   ত + ব = ত্ব

গ + ধ = গ্ধ   জ + ব = জ্ব   ত + ম = ত্ম

গ + ন = গ্ন   জ + ৱ = জ্ৰ   ত + ৱ = ত্ৰ

গ + ব = গ্ব   এঙ + চ = ঞ্চ   থ + ব = থ্ব

গ + ম = গ্ম   এঙ + ছ = ঞ্ছ   থ + ৱ = থ্ৰ

গ + ৱ = গ্ৰ   এঙ + জ = ঞ্জ   দ + গ = দ্গ

গ + ল = গ্ল   এঙ + ঝ = ঞ্ঝ   দ + ঘ = দ্ঘ

ঘ + ন = ঘ্ন   ট + ট = ট্ট   দ + দ = দ্দ

ঘ + ৱ = ঘ্ৰ   ট + ব = ট্ব   দ + দ + ব = দ্দ্ব

ঙ + ক = ঙ্ক   ট + ৱ = ট্ৰ   দ + ধ = দ্ধ

ঙ + ক + ষ = ঙ্ক্ষ   ড + ড = ড্ড   দ + ধ + ব = দ্ধ্ব

ঙ + খ = ঙ্খ   ড + ৱ = ড্ৰ   দ + ব = দ্ব

ঙ + গ = ঙ্গ   ণ + ট = ণ্ট   দ + ভ = দ্ভ

Figure 9. Page 1 of
Assamese conjunct table
keyed phonetically
[typeface: Linotype
Bengali Light] (right).

Figure 10. Example of a
wide character in the
Tamil script [typeface:
Samanti].

could become a reality for non–Latin scripts. Type designs could be true to their cultural heritage.

But the development of non-Latin font libraries has often been in the hands of people who were unconversant with the scripts and who had no sense of their cultural history. Thus in some cases unsuitable designs and errors in letter-formation were translated from one technology to another without correction. Unfortunately,

Figure 11. Example of a
wide character in the
Sinahala script [typeface:
Araliya].

these results are still visible in fonts today due to the economical, and therefore commonplace, practice of converting existing 'acceptable' designs to new font formats.

Digital composition has so far failed to redress the paucity of high quality non-Latin fonts. Few companies have employed teams of skilled researchers, designers, and programmers solely for the purpose of developing non-Latin fonts. Although most non-Latin fonts appear 'calligraphic', with some notable exceptions such as Arabic, there has been scant collaboration between calligraphers and type-designers. Moreover, the well-intentioned drive to facilitate computer-mediated communication in vernacular scripts by standardising and codifying script repertoires (usually by software developers) has not benefited non-Latin typography. The reason is that it does not allow for regional variations, stylistic diversity, or the notion that many non-Latin scripts have no finite character set.[7]

Whilst desktop publishing has empowered personal computer users with font manufacturing software to design and generate their own fonts, in the case of non-Latin scripts it has occasioned a spate of inferior designs. The consequent fonts reveal either a lack of knowledge in a given script, or a lack of training in non-Latin

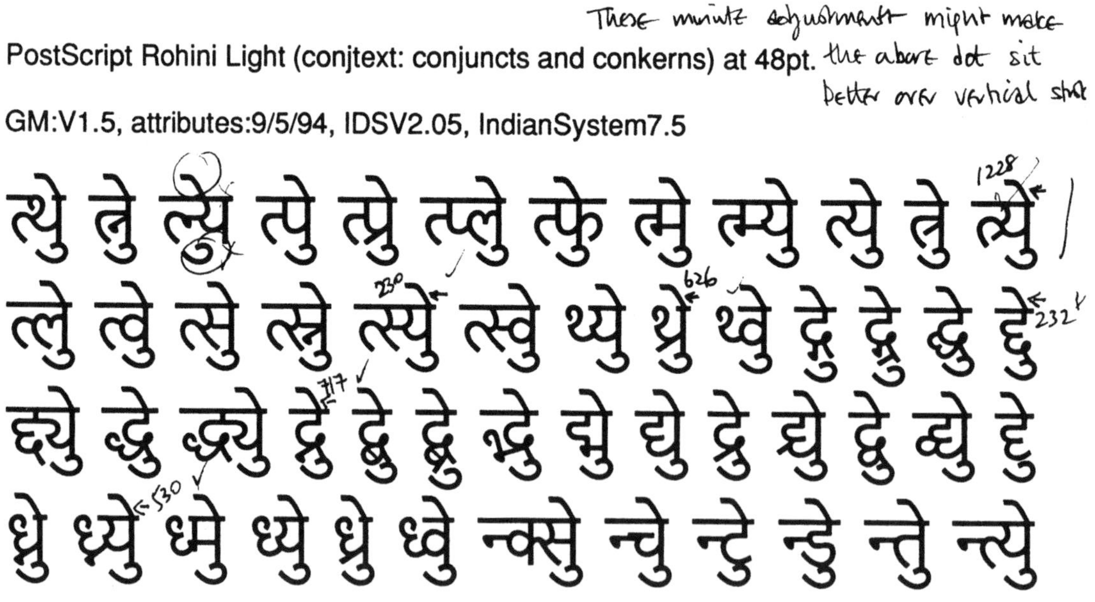

Figure 12. Positioning test of Devanagari monolinear font [typeface: Rohini].

These minute adjustment might make the above dot sit better over vertical stem

PostScript Rohini Light (conjtext: conjuncts and conkerns) at 48pt.

GM:V1.5, attributes:9/5/94, IDSV2.05, IndianSystem7.5

ಕೇಸರಿ

| LIGHT |

ಆನೆಯೊಂದು ದೆಡ್ಡ ಮ್ಯೆಗ. ಅದರ ನಾಲ್ಕು ರೌಲುಗಳು ನಾಲ್ಕು
ಕಂಟಿಗಳ ಥಾಗ ಕಾಣಿಸುತ್ತವೆ, ಆನೆಯ ಕಣ್ಣುಗಳು ಬಹಳಬೆಕ್ಕನಾ
ಗಿನ, ಗೆರಸಿಗಳಹಾಗೆ ಕಾಣುವ ಎರದು ದೊಡ್ಡ ಕಿವಿಗಳು ಆದಕ್ಷಿವೆ.

ಆನೆಯೊಂದು ದೆಡ್ಡ ಮ್ಯೆಗ. ಅದರ ನಾಲ್ಕು ರೌಲುಗಳು
ನಾಲ್ಕು ಕಂಟಿಗಳ ಥಾಗ ಕಾಣಿಸುತ್ತವೆ, ಆನೆಯ ಕಣ್ಣುಗಳು
ಬಹಳಬೆಕ್ಕನಾಗಿನ, ಗೆರಸಿಗಳಹಾಗೆ ಕಾಣುವ ಎರದು

ಆನೆಯೊಂದು ದೆಡ್ಡ ಮ್ಯೆಗ. ಅದರ ನಾಲ್ಕು
ರೌಲುಗಳು ನಾಲ್ಕು ಕಂಟಿಗಳ ಥಾಗ ಕಾಣಿಸು
ತ್ತವೆ, ಆನೆಯ ಕಣ್ಣುಗಳು ಬಹಳಬೆಕ್ಕನಾಗಿನ

| BOLD |

ಆನೆಯೊಂದು ದೆಡ್ಡ ಮ್ಯೆಗ. ಅದರ ನಾಲ್ಕು ರೌಲುಗಳು ನಾಲ್ಕು
ಕಂಟಿಗಳ ಥಾಗ ಕಾಣಿಸುತ್ತವೆ, ಆನೆಯ ಕಣ್ಣುಗಳು ಬಹಳಬೆಕ್ಕನಾ
ಗಿನ, ಗೆರಸಿಗಳಹಾಗೆ ಕಾಣುವ ಎರದು ದೊಡ್ಡ ಕಿವಿಗಳು ಆದಕ್ಷಿವೆ.

ಆನೆಯೊಂದು ದೆಡ್ಡ ಮ್ಯೆಗ. ಅದರ ನಾಲ್ಕು ರೌಲುಗಳು
ನಾಲ್ಕು ಕಂಟಿಗಳ ಥಾಗ ಕಾಣಿಸುತ್ತವೆ, ಆನೆಯ ಕಣ್ಣುಗಳು
ಬಹಳಬೆಕ್ಕನಾಗಿನ, ಗೆರಸಿಗಳಹಾಗೆ ಕಾಣುವ ಎರದು

ಆನೆಯೊಂದು ದೆಡ್ಡ ಮ್ಯೆಗ. ಅದರ ನಾಲ್ಕು
ರೌಲುಗಳು ನಾಲ್ಕು ಕಂಟಿಗಳ ಥಾಗ ಕಾಣಿಸು
ತ್ತವೆ, ಆನೆಯ ಕಣ್ಣುಗಳು ಬಹಳಬೆಕ್ಕನಾಗಿನ

type design. The availability of relatively low-cost font developing tools has also (albeit unwittingly) encouraged typeface piracy, which during the last ten years has rendered investment in new non-Latin type designs an unattractive option for font vendors (figure 13).

However, the increasingly multi-cultural nature of societies worldwide coupled with the typographic potential of the digital era has revitalised interest in non-Latin fonts. Multi-lingual composition is in high demand; and issues of readability are once again of concern, whether for school texts, printed books, vernacular newspapers, screen fonts, or for electronic information interchange. The greater accessibility of font tools, and the typographic possibilities that new font formats promise, indicate that excellence in non-Latin typography in the 'global village' of the third millennium is both desirable and realisable.

Unless otherwise indicated the typefaces mentioned are the property of Linotype Library GmbH. I am grateful to Linotype for the use of typeface material to illustrate points under discussion. Figure 5 is reproduced courtesy of the British Library Board.

Footnotes

1 Discovered in 1966, see Albertine Gaur, *A History of Writing*, (London, 1984), p. 197.
2 Linotype Yakout Simplified Arabic brochure.
3 All of which were re-introduced in the subsequent digital version of the fonts.
4 And continue to be essential, even since the advent of digital technology (see figure 8).
5 See Fiona Ross, *The Printed Bengali Character and its evolution* (Richmond: Curzon Press, 1999), pp. 216-220.
6 Developed by Adobe Sytstems Inc.
7 Or that the writing stystem might still be evolving to deal with transliterating new loan words.

Figure 13. Kanada type specimen [typeface: Kesari] – a font subject to piracy.

EIICHI KONO

English, Japanese and the computer

It seems reasonable to assume that the difficulties experienced in the handling of text for reading and writing might be closely associated with the apparent straightforwardness and logic of the writing system.

Undoubtedly many people share the same view of the simplicity and beauty of the English alphabet. David Diringer with his undoubted scholarship writes in his books, *Writing* (1962, Thames & Hudson) and *The Alphabet* (1948 revised 1968 Funk and Wagnalls, New York): "… with its 22, 24 or 26 signs, the Alphabet is the most flexible and useful method of writing ever invented, and, from its origins in the Near East, has become the nearly universal basis for the scripts employed by civilised peoples, passing from language to language with minimum of difficulty. No other system of writing has so extensive, so intricate and so interesting a history… its use is acquired in childhood with ease. There is an enormous advantage, obviously, in the use of letters which represent single sounds rather than ideas or syllables."

Undoubted facts about the difficulty of learning written English appeared in an article in The *Economist* June 17th 2000: "On June 14th the Department for Education and Employment advertised for a director of a new 'Adult Basic Skills Strategy Unit'. The unit is expected to develop and implement a national strategy to tackle poor literacy and numeracy among adults. By coincidence, on the same day the Organisation for Economic Co-operation and Development published its latest report on 'Literacy in the Information Age'. This demonstrates only too well just how 'poor' literacy levels are in Britain… one in five adults—or about 7m people in Britain—could not find the entry for 'plumbers' in a telephone directory… recent research suggests that… 24% of the population of England are, to varying degrees, 'functionally illiterate'…."

My own experiences are based on learning Japanese as my

mother tongue, and later learning English as a foreign language. As far as I remember I learnt Japanese with ease. As for English, it wasn't difficult to learn ABC, but when it comes to spelling words like 'plumbers' it has been and still is a nightmare to me. I am still definitely 'functionally illiterate'. I don't think that the English alphabet and its use can be acquired with ease. A written English word does not give an immediate visual association with the thing which it represents. I think that picto/idiographic scripts seem to impact on one's mind more directly. I see that the difficulty inherent in learning English is like learning typing with the qwerty keyboard which has been used and loved for a very long time by so many people. It is so well established that it is impossible to change, even though it has obvious functional weakness, and even though better solutions for it have been found. It is entrenched in the whole culture. So is Japanese writing.

During the years since I arrived in England, many people have asked me how my English is getting on, and if Japanese writing is difficult.

Q1. You speak English quite well. How long have you been here?

A1. It's now 26 years.

Q2. What brought you here? What do you do? Where do you work?

A2. I am a graphic/typographic designer working in England. I came from Tokyo to London in 1974 as a mature student studying typography in the English alphabet. I just wanted to learn how to use roman typefaces nicely, not to mention the whims of my mid-career crisis period. While I was still in Japan, I came across some European product catalogues, PR brochures, books, etc. Many of them were beautifully printed in the roman alphabet. And I noticed that the layout with English text produced by Japanese designers and printers did not look as good as the 'foreign' ones, well, the original ones. My ambition grew—to discover good techniques in English typography to bring to Japanese typography, especially for better bilingual setting.

Q3. I see that you speak English well enough. How long did it take you for that?

A3. It took me several years to feel reasonably comfortable in a simple conversation, but I still can't read well, I can't spell, even after 26 years. Maybe that's because I'm a graphic designer!

Q4. Well, English only has 26 letters. How many letters do you use for writing Japanese?

A4. Just about 10,000 appear in the daily newspapers and magazines.

Q5. More than 10,000?! How do you remember them?

A5. I don't remember them all, but I can read somehow. I can guess from the context.

Q6. Are they pictograms like a sign for a toilet, or icons on the computer screen?

A6. Some are. Others are called idiograms, conveying mostly abstract meanings related with the original pictogram; say, a symbol identifying toilets for men or women signifies convenience, necessity or urgency! This is the beauty of *Kanji*. It is possible to understand the meaning of *Kanji* without necessarily knowing the pronunciation.

Q7. It must take ages to write it, musn't it?

A7. Not always. To write 'a mountain' in Japanese *Kanji*, for example, you need four simple strokes. For a 'river', three strokes. Some require many more strokes to write, of course. The *Kanji* for 'depression or melancholy or gloom' needs 29 strokes. Then I try not to write it or not to remember it at all rather than feeling miserable.

Q8. I know reading is easier than writing in English as well. How can you write then if you don't remember them all?

A8. I can substitute with Japanese *Kana*, phonetic scripts which are conceptually a bit like your ABC.

Q9. Do you mean that you have two separate groups of Japanese letters or characters?

Japanese word for 'green' is 'midori'.
It can be written in three ways; with Kanji,
with Hiragana, and with Katakana.
Japanese text is normally written using all
three different kinds of characters.

緑 = みどり = GREEN/green
緑 = ミドリ = GREEN/green
mi do ri

KANJI (ideogram): Basic 1,945 characters + 8,000 or more

HIRAGANA (phonetic script for general use): Basic 46 characters

KATAKANA (phonetic script for foreign words): Basic 46 characters

Green

ROMAN ALPHABET: Basic 26 capitals and 26 lower case letters

A9. The group of pictograms and ideograms which were imported from China around the fifth century are called *Kanji*. The other group of phonetic scripts are called *Kana*, which were subsequently developed around the eighth or ninth century by simplifying the letterforms of *Kanji*. The original Chinese meanings attached to *Kanji* had been dropped, but certain phonetic values were retained to be more suitable for representing Japanese 'HiFi' sounds and for writing more efficiently – just the same way as they, I mean 'we', do now with many imported products. I wonder what Japan would have done to ABC, if ABC had been introduced instead of Chinese *Kanji*.

Q10. My goodness, I am relieved. So, your ancestors had successfully reduced such a large number of Chinese characters to... how many phonetic symbols are there?

A10. 46 or so. Therefore, Japanese can be written entirely phonetically with them. By the way, we have two sets of *Kana*, phonetic scripts (*Hiragana* and *Katakana*). They are a bit like your upper and lower case, so the total is about 92, and some diacritical marks.

Q11. Ours are 26 with which we can do almost everything. Why not use phonetic scripts only? Only 46 (or 92) of them as against 10,000? It's much easier, isn't it?

A11. It's not. Writing Japanese entirely phonetically is cumbersome. The text is hard to read. So we mix *Kanji* and *Kana* together for reading and writing Japanese.

Q12. How do you mix them? Is it because both are insufficient alone so that you have to mix them together? Your simplification technologies in the old days were not as good as the new ones which you often seem to be enjoying, I suppose.

A12. Yes… No… I don't know, but we use them together. *Kanji* are mainly used for the core of words. *Kana* are usually used for grammatical inflection, suffix, prepositions, conjunctions… in a way, they are subordinate.

Q13. It sounds like the Chinese one is better than the Japanese one. I still don't quite understand why it's cumbersome to write all in *Kana*, phonetic scripts instead of complicated *Kanji*.

A13. Please refer to my answers A6 and A7. Writing a word in *Kana* (phonetic scripts) with *Kanji* (picto-ideograms) is often more convenient than just spelling a word only with phonetic scripts or alphabet letters.

Q14. I still don't quite understand why it's hard to read with the simple phonetic scripts like ABC.

A14. Well, a word in Morse code is simpler than a word in ABC. But do you think that the entire text written in Morse code would be easier to read than the text in ABC? Actually, the average mixed Japanese text consists of 30% of *Kanji* (core of word) and 70% of *Kana* (frill of word) … this doesn't mean that Japanese speak mostly frills! Anyway, *Kanji* stands out in the grey sea of the phonetic scripts. These instantly recognisable *Kanji* are very much like icons on the computer screen, so to speak.

Q15. From what you say, it sounds as though our problem with acquiring reading skill in English comes from the fact that the ABC letterform is so simple. But how do they teach reading and writing *Kanji* with such complicated structure and 10,000 or more variations? It must take ages to learn.

A15. We begin with *Kana*, then gradually replace some words in *Kana* with *Kanji*. We are supposed to learn about 1000 *Kanjis* in our primary school – about 1000 more are to be added during higher education. It is said that the total of these 2000 *Kanjis* together with 100 *Kanas* covers more than 98% of everyday Japanese printed matter. They are the essentials.

Q16. So, you really need 2000 letters to read and write. You can give up on the rest of the 8000 or so *Kanjis*, can't you?

A16. Yes, I can. Evidently I have given up since I can't remember even some of the essential 2000. But no, I can't really give them up. The more *Kanji* you know, the more vocabulary you have, because the true nature of *Kanji* is that of word. As you learn more, your vocabulary increases. Anyway, it's always good to realise that learning is a lifetime's work.

Q17. If *Kanji* is a word as well as a letter, 10,000 are not enough for a civilised life, are they? I don't know how many words there are in English, but even the Concise Oxford Dictionary covers 120,000 words.

A17. That's why nobody knows how many Japanese characters exist and how many are necessary. A *Kanji* often conveys important meanings. The combination of *Kanjis* creates further complex meanings. So I guess that the Japanese also have a good number of words like English speaking people.

Q18. It still sounds as though learning Japanese is far more difficult than English. Are many Japanese people illiterate?

A18. I haven't heard that illiteracy is a major social problem in Japan. But I often hear that it is a major problem in Britain. Oh yes, we do have a good traditional Japanese supporting system for reading. Difficult *Kanjis* are often juxtaposed with small phonetic scripts which are called 'Rubi' characters. Many children's books are set in this way. Why don't you do that for yourself? What about using picto/ideographic scripts/symbols as Rubi for phonetically written words? Many icons on the computer screen are accompanied with simple words like a Rubi. By the way, I heard that Rubi derives from 'ruby', an old English type size equal to 5.5 points.

Q19. Why do you think Japan is doing alright in education despite such a complicated writing system?

A19. I don't think it is complicated. It looks complicated. *Kanji* are composed of smaller, simpler units called radicals. 214 radicals are said to be used for *Kanji* as building blocks. Some radicals stand alone as single, meaningful *Kanji*. A radical for 'tree' is a *Kanji* for 'tree' or 'wood' as well. A set of the juxtaposed two 'tree' radicals is a *Kanji* for 'woods'. A set of the three is a *Kanji* for 'forest'. The 'tree' radical and the 'old' radical together make a *Kanji* for 'wither' or 'decay'. A *Kanji* 'woods' and a *Kanji* 'forest' together form a word 'jungle'. A *Kanji* 'tree' and a *Kanji* 'wither' form a word 'wintry wind'. Many English words are also made up with smaller, simpler elements, eg. pre-concept-ion. The idea is the same.

Q20. You put the two 'tree' radicals in parallel for a word 'woods', but you placed the 3rd one on top of them for a word 'forest'. Why don't you put them all in parallel?

A20. There are some rules for positioning these radicals basically in five positions – left, right, top, bottom and the middle.

Q21. I am afraid that you have started complicating the matter again, contradicting the fact that all *Kanjis* can be made with only 214 radicals. How do you remember where to position them? Still worse, the permutation process seems to be done without any reference to the pronunciation.

A21. On the contrary, that seems to be the point for the advantage of using *Kanji*. Compared with the English word which is genuinely phonetic, *Kanji* has more graphic features, which would help us memorise more easily. I think we do it easily because of the human capacity or nature to perceive, remember, categorise and recognise other human faces, and so we do not necessarily need the sound value for it.

Q22. Do you mean that you can read and understand even if you didn't know or remember the pronunciation of some words in the text?

A22. Yes, it is true. Besides illiteracy, dyslexia is the other big problem of yours, so I've heard.

Q23. Yes, that's true. Are there many dyslexic people in Japan?

A23. There are some, but I guess they are very few. I believe so because I haven't come across information about dyslexia in Japan regarded as such a big social issue. I suspect there are as many dyslexic people in Japan as in UK, but they happily escape from being diagnosed as such. They simply don't have to know their potential problem by living in a particular environment, one with *Kanji* in this case. There is an interesting fact: as a result of accident or apoplexy like illness causing the brain damage, there are some Japanese patients who have lost their reading ability, but partially! They become incapable of reading *Kana*, phonetic scripts, but are still able to read *Kanji* which are more complicated in structure than *Kana*.

Q24. 'Less is more' is not always valid, isn't it?

A24. I agree, otherwise you would be starved to death. It reminds me of two different styles in the roman typeface. Serif faces are almost always more in favour for the reading text than sans serif ones. The serifs as an extra visual cue may be contributing to better legibility besides the long-lived familiarity to the reader.

Q25. Are there different styles in the Japanese printing types? Serifs and sans serifs?

A25. There are some equivalents of serif and san serif styles, but not as many as those in English. Designing a font which consists of some 10,000 characters is a big task.

Q26. Now I see your real problem – 'more' is often more problematical. Think about casting metal types for every single font (one style of 10,000 individually different characters in one size). In the case of printing even a simple flyer with a title, headings, sub-headings, regular and bold text, you would need a few million metal types at least. Composition would be another hell, wouldn't it?

A26. It's true. That was how they did it until letterpress printing was gradually (or rapidly) replaced with photo-typesetting and offset–litho process over two decades, and virtually ceased to exist by the mid 1980s. Western letterpress printing was introduced to Japan in the mid 19th century, so that they were doing such absurd things for over a century.

Q27. Were there Japanese private presses in these foolish old days?

A27. I don't think there had been any of that kind if I think about it – the size of an English type case for jobbing work is approximately 80 x 40 cm, but the equivalent for a Japanese one would be three or four cases, the size of a large door. Even tiny printers specialised in printing a business card only, had to have several door-sized type cases in their tiny workshop. These cases were placed against the wall, one on another almost upright, at a slight angle to secure metal types in each compartment, sliding sideways on rails.

Japanese text can be set horizontally as well as vertically (traditional). Set in Heisei-Mincho 11/20pt. English text set in Perpetua 14/16pt.

The riverside near Windsor Castle was in the green of early spring. The river gently meandered, wide and full. It makes me think of the scenes from 'The Complete Angler' by Izaak Walton.

The owner of the riverside house is Hans Schmoller. He was the chief designer at Penguin Books, and many stories have been told about his talents.

ウィンザー城近くの川辺は、早春の柔らかい緑。程よい川幅。豊かな水量、流れはゆるやかに蛇行する。アイザック・ウォルトン、釣魚大全の風景が重なる。

河畔の家の主は、ハンス・シュモーラー氏。ペンギンブックの編集を手がけ、その手腕は数々の逸話で語り継がれている。

ウィンザー城近くの川辺は、早春の柔らかい緑。程よい川幅。豊かな水量、流れはゆるやかに蛇行する。アイザック・ウォルトン、釣魚大全の風景が重なる。河畔の家の主は、ハンス・シュモーラー氏。ペンギンブックの編集を手がけ、その手腕は数々の逸話で語り継がれている。

Q28. A newspaper company must have had an enormous workshop then?

A28. It must have been. Towards the end of 1960s, two major Japanese daily newspapers individually approached IBM to convert their production process into a fully computerised one.

Q29. Didn't they think about photo-typesetting instead?

A29. They thought about it surely. They were desperate to get out of the hellish trap of hot metals. The new photo-typesetting seemed very attractive, but changing the whole system would be an incredibly expensive investment. So they had to think about one more step further – 'what would be after the photo-typesetting?' They were impressed by the US computer technologies able to send their men to the moon. They thought the answer must be somewhere there.

Q30. In what way did they think of using computers for newspaper production?

A30. For typesetting and page layout with digital types on the computer screen, and sending the data for plate making.

Q31. Apple Mac was introduced in mid 1980s. Did the idea of 'digital type' already exist more than fifteen years before that?

A31. It doesn't seem like it. However, these Japanese newspaper companies asked help from an American company who didn't know Japanese language. To the American software engineers, *Kanji* and *Kana* looked like graphic patterns, not letters or characters. That was the key to recognising how type could be made digital.

Q32. How did you know that? When did they succeed?

A32. I read a book called 'The rise and fall in the media industry' written by Takao Sugiyama, published in 1986 by Bungei Shun Shu Co Ltd, Japan. The first newspaper entirely digitally produced was published in March 1978. Around that time, personal computers (PC) were beginning to appear.

Q33. Are PC Windows and Apple Mac popular in Japan? How do they process *Kanji* and *Kana* characters to appear on the computer screen?

A33. Both are very popular. There isn't much difference from processing ABC when you see them working. You can install the Japanese software in your machine to typeset in Japanese as well as English, and do a nice layout. With some sophisticated application programs like the Japanese version of QuarkXpress or PageMaker, you can set the text vertically in its traditional way, or horizontally, by simply selecting the command menu.

Q34. Fine to me, but, I can't imagine the hell it would be to key 10,000 or even 2,000 *Kanji*, or even 214 radicals! How many keys do you need for typing the Japanese text into it?

Input of a word 'midori' using a typical Japanese keyboard.
1. Press keys [m] [i] [d] [o] [r] [i]
   or [key] for switching to Japanese, then [み] [ど] [り]
   (The screen displays みどり)
2. Press [space bar] for conversion
   (The screen displays みどり　ミドリ　緑　美土里　美登里　碧　翠)
3. Use the cursor/mouse to select the desired letter/word, and click
4. Press [return] to confirm

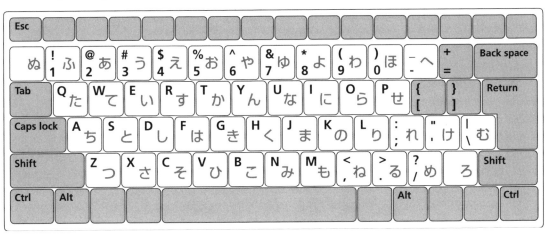

A34. Please refer to my answer A10 – the Japanese can be written entirely with 46 *Kana*. We use the qwerty keyboard, and we use the Romanised Japanese: a roman letter 'a' represents a Japanese vowel 'a'; 'k' and 'a' represents a Japanese *Kana* 'ka'. For example, as you type 'y', 'a', 'm' and 'a' in sequence for a word 'mountain' which is pronounced as 'yama' in Japanese, two *Kanas* for 'ya' and 'ma' automatically appear on the screen. Next you hit the space bar, which automatically brings all the alternative *Kanjis* or words with the same sound value as 'yama'. Then, you choose the one you want by using the cursor or the tab key, and confirm it with the return key.

Q35. Gosh! Still too much to do, isn't it?

A35. The localised qwerty keyboard has keys for *Kanas* as well as for ABC, with which the user needs one key stroke for a *Kana* for 'ya' instead of two key strokes for the same task. In addition, the computer is programmed to adjust itself in some way automatically for the user's preference or convenience. It has a kind of built-in learning capacity for how it's been used, such as your work pattern or frequency. Therefore, two key strokes could be enough for a 'mountain' where you need 8 strokes. Moreover, you would even need 9 or 11 strokes for it if you include a definite or indefinite article. We do not have such articles in our grammar. So, I've heard that the typing speed can be nearly half the speed of that of English. Please watch out! The talking computer will make further big changes.

Q36. Are there many Japanese typefaces? How big is the average Japanese font?

A36. Not as many as in English. Designing a new font which consists of some 10,000 characters is a big task. *Kanji's* complicated structure also limits making variations in weights, proportion, decoration. The electronic size of these fonts would be at least 20 to 30 times heavier than that of the English fonts. The computer is getting more and more powerful, so that this is no longer a problem. These wonderful things have happened to our complicated writing system in the last five years. Japanese is now the second most used language on the Internet, after English.

Q37. You can't beat English to that extent, can you?

A37. No, we can't. Like it or not, English has become the global language. So many different people from so many different places are able to speak, read and write in English to communicate with each other, to get to know each other better, and to get to know one's own language better.

PART 3

CHANGES IN WORK PRACTICES

Book design: before and after
IAN MACKENZIE-KERR BOOK DESIGNER

'Rough ideas for jackets or page layouts which would once have
meant many hours of painstaking work can now be tried out and
discarded in a fraction of the time with an image on the screen
and a printed record of each stage.... For the more traditional
typographer there is a chance to experiment with nuances of
letter spacing and the balancing of type sizes up until the last
possible moment.'

Slouching toward cyberspace: the place of the lettering arts in the digital age
DAVID LEVY RESEARCHER AND VISITING PROFESSOR AT THE
INFORMATION SCHOOL, UNIVERSITY OF WASHINGTON dlevy@lmi.net

'The large-scale adoption of digital technologies is shaking up
the global "ecosystem" that has governed the transmission of the
written word for centuries. It is hard to find a corner of the
world of print that is not experiencing some degree of anxiety
about its future.'

Changes in the relationship between printer and designer: craft before, during and after graphic design
DAVID JURY WRITER, EDUCATOR AND CONSULTANT, HEAD OF GRAPHIC
DESIGN AT COLCHESTER INSTITUTE david.jury@colch-inst.ac.uk

Today, for graphic design students, there is no distinction between
the design process and the craft process. Tacit knowledge has
become a part of conceptual thinking. The craft process creates
knowledge, and the knowlege is applied in the design process.
So much to teach, but sadly so little time to teach it.

IAN MCKENZIE-KERR

Book design: before and after

The words 'Designed and set by...,' which now appear quite often
on the imprint pages of books, would have seemed very surprising
in the not so distant days when the two activities were strictly
segregated and typesetters and designers hardly ever met. The
coming of the computer has meant that many of these relationships
have changed for ever. In the world of book publishing, where
typographical traditions have been observed and cherished for
longer than in many other realms of printing, the impact may have
seemed less obvious. Most of the large number of books published
each week still look much as they have always done. This seems
unlikely to change. But for designers of book jackets or books which
rely on the interaction of pictures and text, which make up an
increasingly large proportion of this output, the new technology has
meant a more streamlined approach, offering exciting opportunities
and occasionally leading to unbridled flights of fancy which would
have seemed equally surprising.

   Typographic design was considered a rather genteel occupation
in my student days at the Royal College of Art in the mid 1950s.
The committed typographers were the ones who brushed their hair,
had clean hands and occasionally wore bow ties. Their tools were
pencils, rulers, layout pads and they carried well thumbed sheets
of type specimens carefully arranged in order. They mostly kept
regular hours and seldom got drunk at parties. There was a small
printing press at the College where our delicately drawn pencil
approximations could be laboriously translated into type, using the
traditional composing stick and a printing process which had hardly
changed since Gutenberg. It was at this time that the mysteries of
typography and the world of print first began to reveal themselves,
becoming at once less abstract and more challenging, and when I
myself, at first rather less commited, began to develop a fascination
for type and its appearance on the page. Given the opportunity to
design a complete issue of the College journal, with the result cast
in metal and staring me in the face, I experienced a sense of

anticipation, tinged with alarm, which has never entirely left me to this day.

Behind this excitement was the realisation that the words, however artfully disposed and beautifully presented, were there to be *read* and that nothing should come between the reader and the message or image on the page. It was also apparent that there were time-honoured conventions attached to the disposition of type, generally recognised and accepted as being inseparable from the printing processes then in use. Unlike the painters and sculptors busily expressing themselves all around us, it was made clear that typographers should aim to be be self-effacing. Beatrice Warde's phrase 'The crystal goblet', her title for a collection of essays on typography published around this time, seemed to sum up the duties and the limitations of the typographer. Even so, there were sometimes doubts and discussions about typographical styles: whether to follow the traditional symmetrical arrangements or whether to be more daring and try the asymmetric styles to be found in the more avant garde publications which occasionally came our way. That some of these more daring styles had been introduced many years before did not seem to make them any less distasteful to the traditionalists or any less attractive to the more adventurous.

Many publishing houses at this time employed a designer, perhaps for only a few days a week. More often the tasks of casting off, marking up manuscripts and specifying typefaces seem to have been handled by the production department or occasionally by the editors. Much was, by tradition, left to the printer, who would often undertake to page the galleys, avoid awkward word breaks and straggling lines and get the whole thing to fit within the allotted space. Illustrations could create problems, especially when integrated with the text, but here again there were many well-tried solutions. There were a number of design-conscious publishers who employed typographers and designers to work on their books and jackets: one thinks of Berthold Wolpe at Faber and Hans Schmoller at Penguin, but there were also many freelance or part-time designers who worked on the increasing number of illustrated books which were starting to appear in the late 1950s and early 1960s, perhaps encouraged by technical advances within the printing industry, but also no doubt due to public demand. Book Design was already being taught as a subject in Art colleges and hopeful graduates were taken on by publishers anxious to extend the range of their lists and branch out into more elaborate books. Book jackets too were becoming increasingly competitive and some booksellers were beginning to display their books in a more imaginative way.

The publishing house which I joined in 1957 had already established a reputation for well-produced illustrated books. My first few weeks were spent coping with a number of minor typographical tasks, in particular a pile of title pages left by my predecessor. I was soon engaged in casting off typescripts in order to assess the length of the text (a skill I never entirely mastered) and preparing carefully drawn out layouts for the printer. The galleys which came back, often many weeks later, had to be cut up and pasted down onto prepared grid sheets. It was a long and often arduous process which required patience and flexibility.
The combined smell of Cow gum and the lighter fuel, which was used to unstick it, lingered in one's nostrils for many days afterwards. Picture material had to be accurately prepared, with precise instructions, for reproduction by metal blocks. Mistakes at this stage could prove expensive, although one could be slightly more relaxed when dealing with offset or gravure. All copies, needless to say, had to be done by hand.

The jackets were mostly designed outside the house, but the typographical matter needed careful attention and could take up a disproportionate amount of time, with several re-settings before everyone was satisfied. It was a familiar working system, common to most publishing houses and relying, like all such systems, on a recognised heirarchy in which the typographer, as distinct from the printer, could be seen to have a small but ever increasing role. The books themselves were becoming more complicated and a number of them were appearing as paperbacks needing separate cover designs.

A foretaste of the new typographical opportunities came in the late 1950s with the introduction of transfer lettering: at first rather limited in its selection and awkward to apply, but soon offering a huge range of types, and particularly display faces, in a variety of sizes. More significantly it offered the designer a new independence from the typesetter and his specimen book, an independence only achieved before by the use of hand drawn letters .

Despite the various portents and rumours which preceded the coming of the computer and its gradual assimilation into the publishing scene it was some time before those of us reared on the disciplines of hot metal and film setting began to realise that we were about to experience a revolution which would, within a remarkably short time, completely alter our working methods. It would have been tempting to stand aside and let others wrestle with the new technology, but rejection would inevitably mean denying oneself the unforeseen pleasure of becoming, in effect, one's own typesetter. We could dispense with pencil roughs. The type would appear before our eyes in whatever size was required, and could be revised with a flick of the finger. Standard type sizes would no longer be relevant (as indeed they had not been in theory since the introduction of filmsetting), and it would now be possible to experiment with half or quarter sizes and the full range of italics, bolds and semi-bolds to achieve the desired balance.

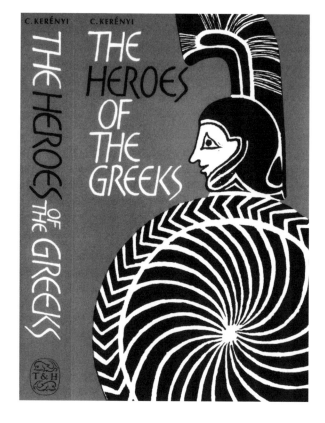

After the initial burst of euphoria at the prospect of this new found freedom two thoughts occured: that typographers themselves could now take on new and daunting responsibilities, and that from now onwards anybody who had access to a computer could try their hand at typographical design. Our rather cloistered occupation would be thrown open to all. Five hundred years of typesetting history and printing practice lay behind us. What could lie ahead?

As far as one can judge the transition seems to have been fairly painless. A generation of computer trained designers has already moved in and job advertisements leave no doubt that this is now a basic requirement. It may have been harder for an older generation, some of whom have probably decided to opt out altogether, but

Two covers from the early 1960s, designed by Ian Mackenzie-Kerr for Thames & Hudson using two colours printed from line blocks. Both use handdrawn lettering. These titles had previously appeared in hardback with more sober jacket designs, and the paperback covers took a rather more playful approach to their serious subjects in the hope of attracting a wider public.

for others, prepared to take the trouble, it must surely have given their working lives a new impetus. Although book publishers do not usually work to the hectic schedules associated with newspapers or magazines, they are often under great pressure to produce visual evidence for advance sales or publicity. Rough ideas for jackets or page layouts, which would once have meant many hours of painstaking work, can now be tried out and discarded in a fraction of the time, with an image on the screen and a printed record of each stage. The opportunities for blending or distorting these images can lead the inventive designer to even greater heights of ingenuity. Storing material on a disk has freed acres of shelf space and saved reams of paper. Increasing familiarity with the computer on both sides can bring editors and designers in a publishing house closer together and, assuming both are willing partners, may lead to a greater understanding of each other's problems.

And for the more traditional typographer, or the more traditional book, there is the chance to experiment with nuances of letter spacing (often a rather chancy business in pre-computer days) and the balancing of type sizes up until the last possible moment. Sir Francis Meynell, who is reputed to have returned title page proofs to the printer many times before he was satisfied, would no doubt have approved.

Many designers would consider these as gains. Have we lost anything in the process? Traditionalists may regret the breaking of the link which often existed between the typographer and the ancient craft of the printer – increasingly, in recent years, separated from that of the typesetter – although experience suggests that this could often be tenuous, the one being slightly wary of the other. It may also be that the young computer-trained typographers have begun to lose the feel for the characteristics of individual typefaces now that there is no longer any need to draw them out by hand. The almost unlimited choice of faces available at the touch of a button and the many graphic devices that the computer has made possible may simply encourage adventurous designers, and perhaps their clients, to attempt novelty for its own sake at the expense of legibility – or perhaps the traditional views on legibility – bearing in mind that perceptions can alter from one generation to the next. The crystal goblet may at times be in danger of overflowing.

The means may have changed but the challenges remain, and the problems faced by the typographer don't go away. Not all of them can be solved by a machine, however sophisticated, although solutions may be reached more quickly. Delays will inevitably occur but they are just as likely to be the result of a technical breakdown or computer failure as from lack of imagination. On these occasions the frustrated designers, assuming that their memories extend so far, may well look back with nostalgia to the bad old days!

Contents page for *Radical Tectonics* in the 4x4 series, designed by Aaron Hayden for Thames & Hudson in 2000, using QuarkXPress 4.1, Adobe Photoshop and Illustrator. An ingenious and intricate design, using the full resources of the computer, which reflects the rather specialized subject matter of the book. A specially created computer generated display face is used as a decorative element.

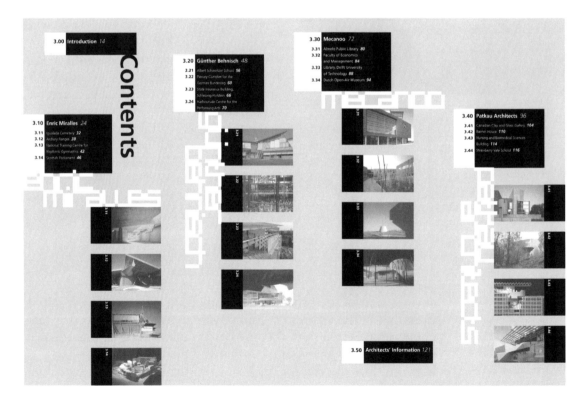

Contents

3.00 Introduction 14

3.10 Enric Miralles 24
3.11 Igualada Cemetery 32
3.12 Archery Ranges 38
3.13 National Training Centre for Rhythmic Gymnastics 42
3.14 Scottish Parliament 46

3.20 Günther Behnisch 48
3.21 Albert Schweitzer School 56
3.22 Plenary Complex for the German Bundestag 60
3.23 State Insurance Building, Schleswig-Holstein 66
3.24 Harbourside Centre for the Performing Arts 70

3.30 Mecanoo 72
3.31 Almelo Public Library 80
3.32 Faculty of Economics and Management 84
3.33 Library, Delft University of Technology 88
3.34 Dutch Open-Air Museum 94

3.40 Patkau Architects 96
3.41 Canadian Clay and Glass Gallery 104
3.42 Barnes House 110
3.43 Nursing and Biomedical Sciences Building 114
3.44 Strawberry Vale School 116

3.50 Architects' Information 121

DAVID LEVY

Slouching toward cyberspace: the place of the lettering arts in a digital era

This article first appeared in the catalogue for *Codes and Messages* 1995, a Crafts Council exhibition curated by Ewan Clayton

The computer may be the best thing that has happened to the lettering arts since Edward Johnston revived calligraphy at the turn of the 20th century.

On the face of it, this claim seems absurd. After all it is widely held that the computer will spell the end of much that the lettering arts community holds dear: paper, handwriting and hand lettering, and that most sacred of artefacts, the book. Or could it be that the current climate offers the lettering arts an opportunity to speak from the margins of our culture?

One thing is clear: we are living through a period of large-scale uncertainty and anxiety. Companies are down-sizing, markets are globalising, once stable nations and economies are crumbling, and once deeply-valued institutions are increasingly treated with suspicion. We are working harder than ever, for less apparent reward, and if we have any time to reflect on our condition (which few of us do), it is only to be puzzled, and perhaps angry, at forces of which we can't quite make sense. There is a general malaise, a sense of rootlessness and dislocation. 'Turning and turning in the widening gyre,' begins Yeats' *The Second Coming,* in one of the most chilling appraisals of the 20th century: 'The falcon cannot hear the falconer;/ Things fall apart; the centre cannot hold;/ Mere anarchy is loosed upon the world,/ The blood-dimmed tide is loosed, and everywhere/ The ceremony of innocence is drowned;/ The best lack all conviction, while the worst/ Are full of passionate intensity.'

Times such as these remind us, somewhat painfully, that the social order, on which so much of our individual and collective well being is based, is a constructed, not a natural, order. Books don't grow on trees, even if they're made from them. National boundaries, cultural practices and social institutions aren't God-given, much as some would like to think. Indeed, even as the underlying chaos is glimpsed through cracks in the social fabric, there is a strong temptation to avert our eyes. 'Pay no attention to the man behind the curtain', says the Wizard of Oz, at the very moment he is being unmasked.

One arena where this dislocation and uncertainty is being experienced on a daily basis is the world of the written word, where the large-scale adoption of digital technologies is shaking up the global ecosystem that has governed the transmission of the written word for centuries. It is hard to find a corner of the world of print that is not experiencing some degree of anxiety about its future. Publishers are wondering whether books will go digital, and if so, how to protect themselves from the wholesale copying of digital works. Librarians are unsure about how to integrate digital materials into their collections and are nervous about whether libraries as we know them will continue to exist. Legislators and lawyers are puzzling over the applicability of current copyright law in cyberspace. Closer to home, many of us still have an uneasy relationship to computers and can't quite make sense of developments like the Internet and the World Wide Web, which are suddenly in the news every day.

There is perhaps some small comfort in realising that we've been here before. In a recent book entitled *The Order of Books,* the French historian, Roger Chartier, points out that it took centuries of work following the introduction of the printing press to 'set the world of the written word in order'. Through what he calls 'an immense effort motivated by anxiety', a range of new structures and practices were invented, including title pages, cataloguing schemes, copyright and the modern notion of authorship. If one wants to imagine how it might have felt to be perplexed and overwhelmed by the quantity and nature of materials pouring off the presses, we might simply reflect on how we feel today in the face of current technological changes. Could it be that we are at the beginning of yet another immense effort, this time to shape and socialise the new forms of documents - among them digital, video and multimedia - that are just beginning to emerge?

But even supposing all this to be so, why should it be of any consequence to the lettering arts, the crafts primarily concerned with the work of the hand, and not of the press or the computer? After all, these crafts were marginalized a long time ago, and have remained on the periphery of current technological and social change. To answer this question, it might be useful to sketch how this marginalization came about.

Before the arrival of the printing press, of course, hand lettering with a broad-edged tool was the method for creating and copying texts. From the late fifteenth century on, as the press gradually displaced the pen, those who wished to make their living as scribes needed to invent a new position for themselves in society. A new profession of 'writing masters' arose who earned their living by teaching others to write a 'fair hand' and by publishing books (printed books!) displaying their own fair hands. (Today's handwriting manuals and 'how to do it' books can be seen as direct descendants of these 'copy books'.) It is from this era, in what we might today think of as a brilliant marketing ploy, that the term 'calligraphy' – from the Greek, meaning 'beautiful writing' – was coined. The OED's first citation for the word is dated 1613.

By the beginning of the Arts and Crafts revival in the late nineteenth century, an understanding of the relationship between the broad-edged pen and the letterforms written with it had been lost. It was left to Edward Johnston to re-articulate how a broad-edged tool could be used to reproduce Western letterforms with simple, elegant, rhythmical strokes. Today, calligraphy is at the periphery of our culture's primary economic and social systems – an integral part of neither the art world nor of publishing and the world of the written word. The other lettering arts are for the most part peripheral in this sense as well.

Calligraphy's marginality is more than just a matter of economics and audience, being also one of values and stance toward the world. In its intent and its practice, it stands at a remove from – indeed in opposition to – some of the directions in which today's technologies are moving us. No one would deny that these new technologies – cellular phones, fax machines, e-mail, the World Wide Web – allow us to cope with lives lived at a faster pace and to keep in touch with one another at vast distances, but in a curious way they seem to exacerbate the problems they aim to solve. Ours is a culture in which people are more fragmented, more disconnected from one another, less in touch with their bodies and their selves. For all our technology, it only seems to be getting worse.

So it is that one of the prices we pay for cellular phones and the like is that we can be interrupted anywhere, anytime. Sustained attention is harder and harder to come by: fragmented awareness is the norm. Our relationship to the material world – the tangible, physical world – is now challenged by the lure of 'virtual reality' and 'cyberspace'. A recent article in *Wired* magazine entitled 'Life in the Digital City' is subtitled 'Pedal down a digital bike path, trawl parks and museums, and find yourself a virtual spouse in new Amsterdam'. And our sense of place is perturbed when any place (the motorway, the bathroom, a restaurant) can be the site of phone discussions and document delivery via fax and e-mail.

But a backlash against these tendencies toward fragmentation, dislocation, and dematerialization is increasingly evident. At the most extreme end are neo-Luddites, who argue for a dismantling of the technological apparatus on which our culture is now built. Within academic circles – and within feminist circles in particular – there is a strong movement to reclaim the place of the body and its embodied wisdom as a source of renewal in science and literature. So-called 'new age' religions are also springing up, attempting to re-establish a more intimate relationship with the earth and borrowing rituals and ideas from indigenous traditions.

The Arts and Crafts movement of a hundred years ago itself arose in opposition to the ethos of its time, in reaction to the perceived disruptive and dehumanizing effects of industrialized mass production. Although it is to this movement that the works in this exhibition most directly owe their existence, their roots actually extend much further back. Indeed, the crafts represented here are part of a continuous, unbroken tradition stretching back many hundreds of years, a tradition concerned with the intimate relationships between people, tools, materials, artefacts and language. It should be obvious that these works are the product of a great investment of time and energy. What may be less obvious is that they have required of their makers a quality of attention, a kind of measured concentration, which can only be found by clearing a reflective, almost sacred, space in which to work. Created in this way, many of the works also ask for a quieter, more reflective reception. They call us to states of concentrated awareness that we are most likely to have encountered in places of worship or in libraries. Both in their making and in their reception and use, these artefacts embody a different rhythm of life – one that is slower, more measured, more rounded. This grounding comes in part from a different attitude and relationship to materials than is the norm in today's disposable society. The materiality of these works is not an afterthought, but a fundamental, inseparable part of what they are. For makers to work with their materials in this way, they must be in touch with their own materiality as well, with their own bodies. The act of writing with a broad-edged pen is an embodied act, which involves the hand, the eye, and more. The calligrapher Donald Jackson often says that the scribe must feel the energy of writing from his toes upward. This is not a metaphor. Such attitudes and qualities as these are hardly the sole property of the lettering arts; they belong to all the crafts. What is distinctive of the lettering arts, however, is their attention to language. The product of the lettering artist's labour is a written artefact, a document. It is easy to lose sight of what remarkable, magical things documents are. Put simply, they are talking things – artefacts in which we have invested a quality we take to be uniquely human, namely, the ability to speak. Documents are very close to us, very much like us. Recall how, in one of the creation stories in Genesis, God forms Adam from the dust of the earth, blowing into him the breath of life. The analogy with the creation of documents is striking and can hardly be accidental. When we make documents, we too take the dust of the earth (clay, stone, plant fibres) and impress into it our voice, which is inextricably connected with our breath. Documents, it seems, are created in our image, as we are created in God's.

In these confusing times, the lettering arts can help remind us where we come from. Perhaps they can also help us shape a better future – but how? Certainly, a neo-Luddite stance is unacceptable; but neither should we settle for an uneasy co-existence with these technologies, like partners in an unhappy marriage. Instead, as we put the world of the written word in order anew, we must work to ensure that, somehow, future documents and document technologies are grounded in the reality of whole, embodied human beings and tangible artefacts.

The digital revolution may thus be a blessing for the lettering arts. By shaking up our institutions and practices, it affords all of us an opportunity – perhaps even forces us – to examine who we are and where we are going. The lettering arts, with their strong stand on people, materials and artefacts, are the carriers of a message that is just as relevant today as in centuries past; it is a message that needs to be heard. But at the same time, the lettering arts are not exempt from the soul-searching and malaise of the day, and they too are called to adapt and grow.

We cannot know whether or not these crafts will make a more central place for themselves in the coming digital era or whether they will continue to speak to us from the margins. But in so far as they speak to our condition (as the Quakers say), we must hope that their voices will be heard.

DAVID JURY

Changes in the relationship between printer and designer: craft before, during and after graphic design

This chapter is based on 'Craft: before, during and after graphic design', an article that appeared in *Typographic* 55 (1999), the journal of the International Society of Type Designers.

The training of the printer in the 'black art' was always a secretive activity, but largely born out of commercial imperative and protection of jobs rather than any concern for the integrity of the craft itself. The 'rules' that might be applied to typography evolved during the five hundred years that the printing trade had a monopoly of all things 'graphic'. These rules were established to expedite the composition of text at a time when printing was labour-intensive and the range of individual competence variable. Rules, therefore, were a necessity to ensure 'house' standards were maintained, that the layout was technically feasible and that the work could be completed within a commercially viable time-scale.

By the end of the nineteenth century, almost all of the printing processes were fully mechanised (1), and there were many within the printing industry who saw its future less and less related to individual craftsmanship (2). The steady increase in scale of manufacturing operations and the resulting loss of personal contact and sympathy of employers to the workforce had slowly strangled the traditional master/apprentice relationship of indentured service (3). After the Second World War, the printing industry seemed eager to make a fresh start. The way forward, echoed at the 1951 Festival of Britain, was to ensure a significant role was established in the growing international markets – the new, 'real' world – and to achieve this fresh start, there were many who felt it had to drop much of its illustrious past. The printing industry, which now often referred to its own workforce as technicians rather than craftsmen, considered science, technology, economics and management studies to be at least as relevant to its future success as the craft skills traditionally associated with quality printing (4). Those who had been trained pre-war in the craft of typography and print, found it particularly hard to adapt. Disillusioned, or fearful of redundancy, a few would change career and work within the education system, perhaps with the sincere hope that their knowledge, firmly based in sound practice, would be used to redress the balance of new technology with that of their own tacit, craft knowledge. However, as typography slowly retreated from the printing syllabus, many would find themselves being asked to pass on their wisdom to the new breed of type user, the graphic design student instead!

In the middle of the twentieth century, the establishment of graphic design (design for print) courses was a direct response to economic demand and technological opportunity. These courses were housed within established art - rather than printing - schools. The immediate dilemma facing these new graphic design courses was that whilst the history of their subject was one based on craftsmanship, the future had been apparently aligned to art (5). In his highly influential book, *Art and Industry*, (1934) Herbert Read argued that the relationship of the artist to the designer was like that of the research scientist to the industrial chemist and physicist. 'In both cases, artists and scientists are concerned with research into the previously unknown, one into the creation of new arrangements of form and colour, the other into previously underdeveloped scientific regions... The results of these discoveries, both in science and art, are then made manifest to a wider public by the industrial scientists, who apply the new facts to practical problems, while the industrial designers and commercial artists make use of new relationships of form and colour to enliven their work.' This view of design's subsidiary or even predatory relationship to art, became a popular and widely held social belief, but it was a genuine source of rancour for designers attempting to establish credibility in a fledgling graphic communications industry, and to graphic design students who were often made to feel distinctly second class to the 'more genuine, more serious' fine art students!

But tensions did not stop there. The establishment of graphic design education in the UK also marked the beginning of a period of acrimonious relations between print and graphic design courses.

A natural resentment quickly built up as printers saw young graphic designers successfully finding work with clients who had previously been the sole preserve of the printing industry. The printing fraternity insisted upon referring to graphic designers as 'artists', a term used with derogatory intent to accentuate the ideological differences between the two. Beatrice Warde was more direct; 'flashy little stylists', she called them. The cause of graphic design education was not helped either by the fact that students appeared to display the worst possible combination of arrogance and ignorance by bringing all traditional typographic 'norms' into question.

Under such circumstances students attempting to extend their understanding of their subject required courage and the acceptance of a highly vulnerable state for themselves. Good design tutors provided enthusiastic support but such students still, inevitably, had to go to the printing school if their layouts were to be turned into reality. As a student in the late sixties, I remember a sympathetic graphics lecturer saying with a wry smile, 'Welcome to the real world...' as I set off down the corridor with layout in hand, to the compositors' workshop. The compositor's view of this situation was described, again by Beatrice Warde, thus: 'The craftsman perceives he is dealing with a pernickety person who has read a book, if not several books, on layout, and owns a pica gauge, and in general has every intention of getting his own way' (6). The graphic design student could not win. If the layout were in any way deficient, he would be told so with brutal candour and sent back to his studio with a clear if unspoken message for his tutor. Alternatively, if it were 'insultingly precise... the kind which gives the the executant no chance whatever to "use his head"'(7) the student was accused of insulting the compositor's intelligence and ignoring his craft skills. This would not actually be said, of course, because to admit as much would, in itself, be demeaning. So the very best a graphics student could expect – if the obligatory oral examination had been passed – was a display of mock subservience, '...and when was the young master-typographer hoping to see his proofs?'

I was intrigued by the apartheid that existed between the design studio, the 'thinking' area, and the printing workshops, the 'making' area. Of course, this simplistic model does not do justice

to either but for a student the cultural differences between the two
meant that you really had to align yourself with one camp or the
other, making a thorough and intelligent understanding of
typography virtually impossible.

Not surprising then, that Letraset, widely available as a dry-
transfer product by 1965, proved to be so popular amongst graphic
students. The reason for this was simple: it liberated them from the
print school. Nothing needed to be explained, justified or apologised
for. Suddenly typography was easy! Letraset was a highly 'flexible'
medium, allowing endless distortion of letterforms and total
freedom regarding alignment and spacing. The results were viewed
by many as proof that typographic standards had sunk to an all-
time low as students, left to their own devices, appeared to display
their total ignorance of (or simply chose to ignore) typographic
craft. Looking back, even at professional work produced at the
time, I can understand the concern. Letraset was a rather crude
product and its physical characteristics encouraged students to use
the distortions inherent in the product for shallow 'expressive'
reasons. Used once and the distorted plastic 'carrier' sheet would
make accurate inter-character spacing impossible, so it became
normal practice to space characters so close as to create words
made up of one continuous ligature. The old rules could not be
applied, so new ones were created.

In many ways, with its flexibility of application, relative
cheapness and its democratising influence, Letraset had many of the
characteristics which computer technology would bring twenty
years later. But with the computer there arrived a technological
revolution with far wider implications, since it destroyed the
barriers that had traditionally separated the roles of the designer-
typographer and the printer. The whole 'typographic' process had
suddenly become one singular activity and the printer found that
'type', which had been synonymous with 'print' for the previous
500 years, had been rudely snatched away and delivered, wrapped
in a portable new machine, and dropped into the lap of the graphic
designer. The printer had become the hod carrier, the graphic
designer, that flashy little stylist, the architect (8).

The effect of computer technology upon design education has
been profound, but is somewhat distorted (to its detriment) by the
coincidental arrival of radical, government-led policy changes

which have had far-reaching consequences for the delivery of higher education (9). One of the most obvious elements, certainly for design education, has been sweeping financial cuts, resulting in a reduction both in the number of lecturers and in the number of hours available to teach. Most design courses at higher education level now offer final year students less than fifteen hours contact teaching, which is two and a half days of standard college time (10). The paucity of tutor contact will be justified to students as 'time to reflect' or to encourage 'self-management skills'. Not surprisingly, those students who can afford it will buy their own computer and work at home on all days when not required to be in the college studio or at lectures. Indeed, it is not unusual for students to arrive in time for a tutorial and then immediately disappear once that particular session has finished. The limited access to the computer suite and the inevitable pre-booking system often makes it difficult for the student to justify spending money travelling into college when there is a computer available at home.

This tendency to work alone demonstrates both the strength of the computer and its weakness, certainly from an educational point of view. Just as the students in the sixties found Letraset a liberating medium because they no longer needed to seek the aid and approval of the print department, so today, the computer allows this situation to go one stage further – students can now work at home producing a 'completed' solution without contact with any tutors.

Before computers, tutors could keep up with the progress of each individual student because the design process could be identified by physical results and the typographic elements required easily identifiable pre-planning and the writing of lucid specifications. The design process was slower and generally took place on a large table-top in full view of tutors and the peer group, providing time and space to discuss progress and the possibilities of appropriate alternatives. This was, essentially, a craft activity. To 'mock-up' even the simplest piece of printed matter would require research into materials and processes involving reading, talking to people, and the skilful manipulation of papers, boards, drawing instruments and various drawing media, measuring, cutting and gluing. It also involved planning since the activity entailed a risk of irreversibility if things went wrong. In better students all this instilled a determined physical dexterity, mental rigour and a devotion to personal expression. However, in weaker students, a distinct tendency to play safe and repeat what worked last time would be the norm.

Arts and crafts are identified as much by material as by practices or modes of expression. The workings of these materials has been the source of a greater, tacit knowledge. However, it is a characteristic of the computer that, potentially, every printout, achievable at the press of a button, is the 'finished' item, and unless the student has the knowledge (and the time and will-power) to question what the computer has provided they will accept that the job is, indeed, finished. Prior to computers the solution would need to be 'made' – a process which enabled discussion, argument and the opportunity to voice opinions which, in itself, enriched the craft process by allowing alternatives to be considered right up to the end.

Letraset was never a threat to the compositor; by its nature it could only be used effectively for headlines. The computer, however, having eliminated the need for a compositor or typesetter, places the burden of typographic responsibility squarely with the designer. The 'black art' of making words readable has got to be learnt by graphic designers. A glance in any bookshop will immediately tell you that this is not happening. The typographic 'rules' referred to in this article and established by generations of printing craftsmen have been not so much questioned as almost forgotten. These were the result of accumulated knowledge concerning the very essence of graphic communication and contained a great deal of common sense. However, sitting at a computer; moving, tilting, blending, reversing, polarising, filtering, layering, grading, fading, extending and condensing anything and everything at the move of a mouse and the press of a button, it is not surprising that students, when questioned about what they are doing will say: 'Rules... what rules?' Until very recently, it was possible for graphic design courses to skirt around this detailed, pernickety aspect of typography in the sound knowledge that the textual detail would be picked over by somebody else. This is no longer the case. The tragedy of it all is that the computer offers far more, almost infinite control over textual detail, and certainly far more than any previous technology.

The failure of graphic design courses to adequately address this issue has encouraged some to argue that typography is too important to be left to designers (11). It is argued (quite rightly) that the typographic designer needs a broad knowledge of communication theory, linguistics, semiotics and information technology. Most Humanities faculties offer these subjects plus media and cultural studies, and, as often as not, professional writing. There are already courses – with typography in the syllabus – in multimedia, broadcasting and publishing being taught by lecturers with no training whatever in graphic design.

Warnings have been regularly sounded since the sixties. The UK Working Party for Typographic Teaching (WPTT) in 1968 recommended, '... the typographer has much to learn from the new discipline of linguistics, which is concerned with the study of the function and structure of language in general. Typography can legitimately be seen as "visual linguistics" and should be studied in relation to the wider use of language.' (12). In 1972 Weingart said, 'Certainly in the future, a study of typography must include a study of the meaning of "text"… we will need input for new fields such as: sociology, communications theory, semantics, semiotics, computers and planning methods.' (13). Recently, there has been a plethora of how-to-do-it books on website design and desktop publishing which explain on their covers that 'No graphic design skills are necessary'!

Computers have speeded up the process of design, but this is not, in itself, a bad thing. The problem is that, coincidentally, the amount of available time to teach has been reduced when logically it should have been increased. The computer has also delivered a whole new area of graphic design which is not being addressed adequately, namely textual design. Craft and typography, as part of the graphic design curriculum, is being squeezed out as studio spaces are reduced and computer suites expanded. In fact, studio culture, once the mainstay of design education, is in danger of disappearing altogether. If we are serious about developing creativity in particular, and human knowledge in general, we have to maintain the rich and diverse physical as well as mental activities associated with the exploration and production of graphic communication. In the present climate this is difficult to imagine.

I do not want to advocate separating 'typographic' design from 'graphic' design. Typographic design can, and does, benefit greatly from the designer's wider knowledge (and pleasure) gained by engaging in activities that might be described as tactile, hands-on, messy, or simply 'craft'. But arguments for a more 'scientific' approach to typography, perhaps offered by alternative non-visual courses, are going to become more and more difficult to resist unless graphic design courses cover this aspect of the curriculum adequately. Otherwise, the burgeoning technology will allow the subject to be snatched away from the graphic designer just easily as it was snatched away from the printing industry. Without typography, 'flashy little stylists' would be an appropriate description of what's left of the graphic designer's role.

References

1   Michael Twyman. *Printing* 1770–1970. The British Library 1998.

2. See J R Riddle (Principal of the London College of Printing). Training the Printer of the Future. *Monotype Recorder* pp.10–11. 1928.

3. Until the mid-seventies 'The British Printing Industries Federation' (BPIF) had been named 'The Federation of Master Printers' (BFMP).

4. 'The printing industry believes it will need more technologists and technicians before the full potential of all recent and future developments can be attained... [A printer's training] in science, technology, economics and management subjects enables them to render valuable assistance... so even the smaller firms find it profitable to make use of their services.' G F Caldwell. Future Pattern of Printing Education. *Penrose Annual* Volume 55, 1961.

5. James Holland. The Art School Dilemma. *Penrose Annual* Volume 59, page 162, 1966.

6. Beatrice Warde, *The Pencil Draws a Vicious Circle, The Crystal Goblet*. The Sylvan Press, 1955.

7. Ibid.

8. Ibid.

9. David Jury, Purchasing Power, *Graphics International,* February 1999.

10. The first course I taught on – an Ordinary National Diploma

(OND) course in graphic design in 1980 – was allocated 32 hours per week, and included two evening classes.

11. Cal Swann, Typography is too important to be taught to designers, *TypoGraphic* 49, 1996.
12. The Working Party for Typographic Teaching (WPTT) clearly aligned itself with the latter. For the full WPTT Interim Report written under the chairmanship of Michael Twyman see *TypoGraphic* 52, page 6, 1996.
13. Wolfgang Weingart, How can one make Swiss typography? *Octavo* 87 – 4.

Acknowledgments

Peter Dormer, *The Art of the Maker: Skill and its meaning in Art, Craft and Design*, Thames and Hudson, 1994.

Lorraine Wild, 'That Was Then: Corrections and Amplifications', *The Education of a Graphic Designer*, edited by Steven Heller. Allworth Press, 1997.

All Our Futures: Creativity, Culture and Education. Report by the National Advisory Committee for Creative and Cultural Education, 1999.

PART 4
LETTERFORMS AND THE COMPUTER

Hand, eye and mind: a design trinity

MICHAEL HARVEY, LETTERERING DESIGNER, perdido@dircon.co.uk.

Anyone who designs, draws or carves letters, or creates them digitally, needs to understand their shapes, how each character arrived at its particular form.

Metafont in the Rockies: the Colorado typemaking project

RICHARD SOUTHALL, COMPUTER–TYPOGRAPHER AND RESEARCHER, richard@typo.demon.co.uk

In the Colorado project (typefaces designed for telephone directory composition on laser imagesetters), fontmaking with metafont made three things possible that, in the context of the time, seemed hard or impossible by any other means.

MICHAEL HARVEY

Hand, eye & mind: a design trinity

In the autumn of 1999, a book called *The Hand* came into my hands which reinforced much of what I knew from long experience in making letters with pencil, pen, brush, chisel and mouse. The author of this study of the hand's place in human development, Frank R Wilson, summed up his thesis with the subtitle: How its use shapes the brain, language and human culture. Using our hands to make things – which, to Wilson, a gifted pianist, includes music – develops an area of the brain untouched by any other activity. Here was a book that, through historical and scientific evidence backed up by case histories of patients treated by Wilson, put into words what I had discovered through my own work but had barely articulated.

This discovery was a long time coming. After thirty years as a lettering designer that included drawing letters for many purposes, I wrote *Creative Lettering: drawing & design*. In this book I described what, for me, drawing letters freehand involved. I thought I knew, but to make sure I mounted a camera over my hand to record the sequence of finger movements as I drew. When studying the images I had evidence of how my fingers exercised a remarkable yet mostly unconscious control of the lines that made up each character – lines as personal to me as my handwriting. The subtitle of my 1975 book on lettering design, *Form & skill in the design & use of letters* hinted at what I had now discovered.

The shapes of letter forms are largely controlled by convention (the need, usually, to be legible), and also affected by practice and fashion. They create a visible language that ranges from the most austerely beautiful capitals to the wildest scripts. The roman capital is itself hidebound by convention, its forms apparently unalterable, yet, as I discovered, by drawing these forms directly, letting my fingers shape each character while my eye (and mind) kept watch on the emerging shapes, these classic, timeless letters acquired an extra, indefinable quality which can only be called individuality. This was not a contrived effect, not a conscious styling. That would be affectation. I had found that even letters as ruled by convention as these, may acquire a quality imparted unintentionally by their maker. How else do we recognise, say, a typeface by Hermann Zapf? Some individual quality speaks to us that can only come from his hand, his eye, his mind.

Letters are only forms, shapes before we learn their names and relationship to other forms and shapes. That is the case when we are young and know nothing of their unique importance in the visible world. As a boy I drew what excited me: aircraft, locomotives, ships under sail. I was excited by their shapes as much

Illustration from 'Creative Lettering: drawing & design', London 1985

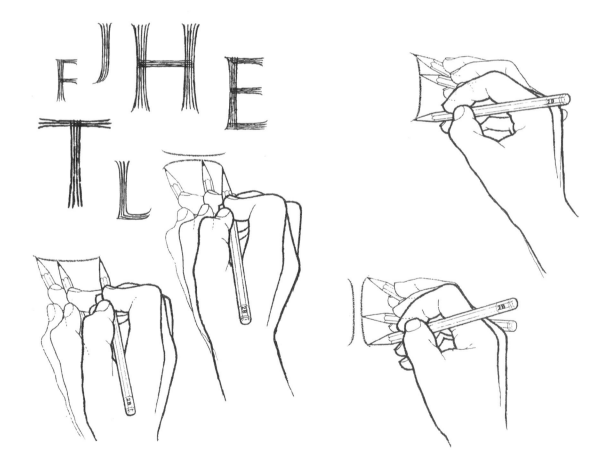

Drawing for book cover
'Meisje in de winter',
Amsterdam 1984

Philip Larkin Meisje in de winter

Philip Larkin

Meisje in de winter

ROMAN

as by their actions. They were worth making drawings of. It was the same feeling when making model aircraft, shaping the fuselage and wings with a razor blade in balsa wood, trying to get the shapes right. I am sure now that this early experience in making has been an important and invaluable thread in my later professional work. It's all shaping, whether it's a Spitfire's wing in wood or a letter S carved in stone.

Anyone who designs, draws or carves letters, or creates them digitally, needs to understand their shapes, how each character arrived at its particular form. Without such understanding their rendering of the alphabet will lack conviction, and the essential

DUKE ELLINGTON, BANDLEADER, COMPOSER AND PIANO PLAYER,
DESCRIBED HIS MUSICAL EVOCATION OF LIFE IN A TENEMENT
BUILDING IN HARLEM AS FOLLOWS . . .

. . . and take my *Harlem Air Shaft.*

So much goes on in a Harlem air shaft.

You get the full essence of Harlem

in an air shaft. You hear fights,

you smell dinner, you hear

people making love.

You hear intimate gossip

floating down.

YOU HEAR THE RADIO.

AN AIR SHAFT

IS ONE GREAT BIG

LOUDSPEAKER.

You see your neighbours' laundry.

You hear the janitor's dogs.

The man upstairs' aerial

falls down and breaks

your window.

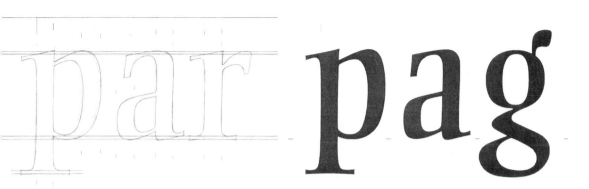

Character drawings for
Ellington type face
(Monotype 1990)

Opposite: Ellington
type specimen
(Monotype 1990)

practice here is writing with the broad-edged pen. Such practice is similar to that of an actor who learns Shakespearean roles, acquiring a basic discipline before moving with confidence into other branches of the theatre. In the same way a designer of letters may begin by concentrating on roman capitals and the main scripts: uncial, minuscule, blackletter and italic, before tackling other letter-making skills and forms. It is not necessary that the person getting to grips with writing tools become a calligrapher – that branch of letter-making requires long and intensive practice – but rather that they acquire an insight into letterform development and construction. Through learning by doing, hand skills are formed and an intuitive, felt experience of letters is established. The eye, too, has its perceptions refined, its ability to discern good from less good, its critical faculties heightened.

Engraving is a little appreciated skill and its influence on letters is undervalued. As type replaced writing, the engraver of punches replaced the scribe as a maker of letters – letters that were increasingly for general consumption as literacy spread with the printed book. The difference between the scribe, whose marks swiftly fill lines and pages with alphabetic text, and the punchcutter who slowly shapes individual letters in steel could not be more marked. Beginning in the early days of printing, the engraver of punches, as a reproducer of written characters, transformed the shapes he made in steel into true typographic letters and these lost virtually every characteristic of the broad-edged pen. The typefaces of Bodoni and Walbaum exemplify this transformation. Apart from the changes noted above there was also the fact that whereas the scribe's letters flowed one from another to make words, the engraver worked on individual letters one at a time. His work was part of a process in the making of type letters that were later assembled into text. With the so-called copperplate scripts of the eighteenth century a dramatic change in style and form is evident. Pen and graver vied with each other in making elaborately flourished designs.

The importance of drawing is little appreciated, in either letter-making or in the wider world of manufacture. It is a fact that the whole industrial revolution depended on drawing, on the skills of the engineering and architectural draughtsman. Drawing brought the order and technical precision on which ship building, railways, the manufacture of locomotives and other machines depended. The spread of architectural styles across Europe and America since the Renaissance would not have been possible without drawings. As typefaces in many styles and weights proliferated during the nineteenth century, emerging from the burgeoning type foundries drawing must have been part of the process, at least in the design stage. The mechanically exact forms of the new sanserif letters certainly show this. When punch cutting was taken away from the individual engraver and transferred to machines, the drawing offices of type foundries assumed a major role in type production by providing the precise character drawings from which the patterns that the machines followed were made. Type designers now became separated from type production, and their names began to become well known. An obvious example is Eric Gill. His designs for Monotype began with his drawings which were then developed by the company's large staff of draughtsmen and women to give them the critical precision required to fit the Monotype casting system. A close look at Gill's originals shows how much was lost in this process, yet the types retain his character. As well as technical drawing, which relies on instruments like compasses, set-squares and such, there have always been freehand drawn letters: one thinks of the inventive initials in early manuscripts, and more recently the art nouveau letter of the late nineteenth century, the graphic letters in twentieth-century advertising, and the work of those artists who have used letterforms in their images.

The letter-making skills described here ignore the wider cultural factors that have influenced the Western alphabet's development –

but we can leave this to the historians. At the University of Reading's Department of Typography & Graphic Communication the course on letterforms has introduced these skills in short sessions to help students understand why letters are the shapes they are. Students use brushes and pens to recreate capital letters and the main scripts, learning how these forms were made, even though they mostly lack the necessary skill. Engraving is simulated with lino-cutting to show how script forms are translated into engraved forms, and punch cutting is experienced on a large scale with wood and wood carving tools. Later in the course students use technical drawing to construct letters, then draw freehand to explore other graphic letterforms. A session of letter carving in stone precedes a final study of digital letter design on screen. At the end of these six sessions, in which several skills have been briefly experienced, students have gained first-hand knowledge of character design and development. Complementary lectures on the history of lettering given by James Mosley supply the rest of the story.

According to Frank R Wilson, some high-tech corporations in the United States require applicants for positions to show some evidence of hand skills as well as computer expertise, reasoning that the benefits that hand work brings in judging digital images are an essential qualification. And Eric Hobsbawm, writing about the replacement of the skilled manual worker by the machine in Victorian times, says: 'What will a country be like without the road to self-respect which skill with hand, eye and brain provide for men – and, one might add women – who happen not to be good at passing examinations?' Finally, here is an extract from my letter to *The Independent* which was a response to another correspondent who said that children should learn 'how to express ideas and information properly, and leave calligraphy as an option in the handcraft syllabus'. 'Learning to write', my letter said, 'brings with it an appreciation of those fundamentals of the visual world: line, form, space and pattern. The visual illiteracy of the average person today may be partly due to not having learnt to write decently.'

RICHARD SOUTHALL

Metafont in the Rockies: the Colorado typemaking project

The paper describes the task of making fonts for a new family of typefaces designed for telephone directory composition on laser image-setters. A key requirement for the font production method was that the visual relationships between the design variants used for the different components of directory entries should be precisely controllable over a range of character image sizes. The factors leading to the decision to program the character shape specifications explicitly, rather than taking the more normal approach of numerical contour capture, are discussed. Knuth's Metafont, employed in a somewhat unconventional way, was used as the font programming language.

This article originally appeared in *Electronic publishing, artistic imaging and digital typography* (1998) edited by Roger D. Hersch, Jacques André and Heather Brown. The article appears here by permission of Springer-Verlag.

1 Background

US West Dex (USWD) is the directory-publishing arm of US West Inc, a telephone services provider in the western United States.

US West's territory comprises 14 states, extending from the Canadian to the Mexican border and from Iowa in the east to Oregon in the west. USWD produces directories in a wide range of formats to cover this variety of terrain. A typical directory for a metropolitan area such as Denver or Seattle has a residential white-pages section of somewhere between 1000 and 1500 pages, with around 460 entries per page. At the other extreme are small-format rural-area directories with white-pages sections of 70 or 80 pages, each with around 120 entries in which residential and business listings are combined. In between are directories for many areas of intermediate size; the larger ones tend to have residential and business entries listed separately, while the smaller ones combine them. A typical example for a medium-sized area has 234 large-format pages of residential listings, with an average of 246 entries per page.

There is a growing trend for the large metropolitan directories to be supplemented by 'community directories' with smaller page formats, covering part of the larger area. A typical directory of this type has 602 pages of residential listings, with an average of 186 entries per page.

Only the metropolitan directories have separate volumes for white and yellow pages; in all the other directory types the two are bound up together.

US West is bound by the regulatory regime under which it operates to provide white-pages directories to its customers free of charge. These directories are not a source of revenue for USWD, and there is a considerable commercial incentive to reduce their production costs. By far the largest component of these is the cost of paper, so that the most effective way to reduce costs is to reduce the number of pages by increasing the number of entries per page. The cost saving per page saved will be proportionately greater in the metropolitan and community directories, which are printed in large numbers. US West is also obliged to furnish its customer listings to anyone prepared to pay for them, and since money can be made from charging for supplementary entries there is competition in directory provision: once again, primarily in metropolitan areas.

In redesigning directories in such an environment, the commercial objectives are therefore to make the new directories have fewer pages than they did before, and to be easier to read than the competition's.

2 Early Work

In the first months of 1995 Ladislas Mandel, a well-known French type designer who has produced many typefaces for telephone-directory work (*cf.* Mandel 1978) was contacted on behalf of USWD with a request to prepare a proposal for new typeface designs for their directories. At that time it was envisaged that imagesetters with comparatively low resolutions, of 1016 or even 900 dots per inch (dpi), would be used to produce photo-composed output. Mandel in turn contacted me, since he knew I had experience of font production in low-resolution environments.

In our first discussions, Mandel was emphatic about the degree of control over typographic parameters such as stroke-weight and character spacing that he wanted in the finished fonts. Much of his early directory work had been for cathode-ray tube (CRT) photo-composing machines, such as the Autologic APS series. In these, a single bitmap font is made to provide character images over a size range of around 4:1 by varying the deflection sensitivity of the electron beam and consequently the writing resolution of the device (Seybold 1984, ch. 9). In a system of this kind the designer has complete control over the configurations of the character images. The machine imposes no interpretations of its own on the information contained in the font.

Needless to say, laser image-setters do not work like this. In normal practice, the fixed-resolution bitmaps the image-setter writes for each character image size are produced by separate rasterisations of a single set of outline character shape specifications, with all the possibilities for inconsistency of stroke-weight and spacing that present-day font formats are designed to minimise. It appeared from our conversations that Mandel's experience with outline renderings of his designs had been uniformly bad. He would not acknowledge that PostScript fonts could ever perform as he wished them to, and looked to me to provide an alternative.

Mandel insists on accurate control of typographic parameters because the different variants in his directory typeface families are designed to work together in precisely defined visual relationships. This has another consequence as well: there have to be enough pixels in the em square of the output size to accommodate the differences in character stroke-weights that are needed to give a proper rendering of the intended differences in visual weight between the variants.

In low-resolution environments, this consideration imposes a lower limit on the image sizes that can be composed. For the USWD designs, Mandel wanted an em square of at least 89 pixels. At 1016 dpi this equates to a nominal size of 6.33 pica points, larger than is desirable or necessary for directory setting. In his original proposal to USWD Mandel therefore envisaged photographic reduction of composed pages to a nominal type size of 4.5 pt from camera-ready copy produced at 6.33 pt on 1016-dpi machines.

3 Font-making Methods

With this in mind, Mandel began preparing character designs on an 89-square grid. At the same time I began to review the options for font production, using as specimen material some drawings provided by Mandel of his Clottes typeface, which he had designed for use in France Telecom's A5-format 'mini-directories' at 3.3 pt Didot (approximately 3.5 pica points).

One alternative was to follow Mandel's thinking and produce a single set of bitmaps for each variant in the 89-pixel size. These could be realised as PostScript Type 3 fonts to satisfy USWD's raster image processors (RIPs), which only accepted PostScript input. However, at a meeting in July 1995 the possibility was raised by USWD that direct-to-plate composition might be introduced in the medium term for directories with relatively short print runs. Such directories very often contain combined residential and business listings, in which different type sizes are mixed on the same page. It thus became clear very early in the project that no font-making solution that restricted output character images to a single size would fulfil USWD's actual requirements except in the very short term, and perhaps not even then.

At this point the obvious course might have appeared to be to render Mandel's drawings with conventional techniques of numerical contour capture and onscreen hinting, to produce a set of PostScript Type 1 fonts. However, there were a number of reasons that dissuaded me.

For one thing, as already mentioned, Mandel wanted to control the differences between the stroke-weights and the counter widths of the different variants in the finished fonts.[1] These differences were expressed on his drawings in terms of pixel counts, and I knew he would want to check them in the same terms on any proofs that might be produced. I was not certain that the resources provided by Type 1 hinting would be adequate to meet this challenge reliably at the small pixel sizes with which we were concerned.

Related to this was the question of rasterisation effects. On the comparatively coarse pixel grids we were dealing with, rasterisation necessarily distorts the configurations of characters to some extent. Taking small h from the light condensed variant of the new design as an example, vertical stroke-weights of 8 pixels on the 89-pixel square scale arithmetically to 7.55 at 84 pixels, which is 6.0 pt at 1016 dpi. The counter width of 20 pixels scales to 18.88. Normal rasterisation rounds the stroke-weights back to 8 and the counter

1 Counters are the interior spaces of characters, for example between the upright strokes of small n.

width to 19 pixels, so that the proportion of counter width to stroke-weight decreases by 5% with the change in size. I wanted the option of maintaining the counter width at 20 pixels in the smaller size, and doing the same with the other variants, to preserve the visual differentiation between them.

This requirement is in fact an aspect of the more general issue of non-linear scaling. Following Harry Carter and Walter Tracy (Carter 1937; Tracy 1986, Ch. 6), as well as Mandel's views and my own, I anticipated that we would need to widen the counters of the USWD characters relative to the weights of vertical strokes, as well as rounding the stroke-weights upwards as character image-size decreased.[2] The same mechanism, hypothetical as yet, that compensated for rasterisation effects could also be used for this task.

With hindsight, I can see that the control value tables of TrueType would have offered solutions for all these problems. However, at the time my ignorance of the language was matched by that of USWD's RIPs, which did not understand it either.

Quite apart from these issues of stroke-weight differences and character proportions, however, was another consideration that appeared to rule out any contour-based approach completely (although, once again, I now know that TrueType could probably have solved it). We wanted some parts of the character shape specifications to be scaleable, and others not.

This requirement comes from the nature of telephone-directory publishing, which in many ways resembles classified-advertisement publishing in newspapers. Newspaper classifieds are made small to maximize revenue, and directory entries to minimize cost; but the technical requirements are very similar in the two cases. The size of the type means that great craft and skill are needed to maintain its legibility;[3] long print runs, high web speeds, inexpensive paper and thin ink mean that the character images on the printing plates must be physically robust.

In his work for CRT photocomposing machines, Mandel had taken advantage of the control over character image configuration the technology gave him to add pixel-scale features to his designs that increased their robustness. Examples of such features are finials

---

2 This is not exactly what happened in the event: see Fig. 4 below.
3 Mandel had indeed designed a series of classified-advertisement typefaces for International Photon in the 1970s.

at the squared ends of strokes, and cutouts or rebates at right-angled interior junctions. These are put there to be sacrificed during typesetting and printing, leaving behind them the 'real' intended shape of the character. Without finials or cutouts, square stroke ends would become rounded and interior junctions fill in.

Because they are not part of the character shape, features of this kind should not scale with the rest of the shape specification. Their dimensions depend on the magnitude of the effects for which they are intended to compensate. These are absolute, in terms of radii on the photographic material or distances on the printing plate, rather than relative to the dimensions of character images. A one-pixel-square cutout should remain one pixel square, whatever the size of the image of which it forms a part. I could not see how to achieve this behaviour with PostScript outline specifications.

Taking all these factors into account, I concluded that the character image specifications in the USWD fonts would need to be explicitly programmed. A choice of programming language therefore had to be made.

Although in principle the field was open between PostScript and Metafont, with TrueType on the outside, in practice there was no contest. I had worked with Metafont at Stanford and Strasbourg in the 1980s (Southall 1985, 1986) and knew that it would respond to all of Mandel's requirements. The language was well suited to his methods of working, since it allowed the use of both image-related and absolute dimensions. Although my earlier work had not resulted in a completed typeface, it had produced a number of useful tools for font development: in particular, procedures for printing out enlarged views of the pixel configurations of characters in the fonts (Fig. 1) and the outlines from which they were derived. I had also made use of the elegant technique for non-linear scaling of character dimensions devised by John Hobby (Knuth 1986b, Appendix D).

I wrote Metafont programs for the Clottes characters which performed well – both at the 89-pixel size and at sizes down to 38 pixels (9 pt at 300 dpi; 2.7 pt at 1016 dpi). These tests showed that consistencies of character proportion could be preserved across a range of pixel sizes. They told us nothing, however, about the problems of mixing different weights.

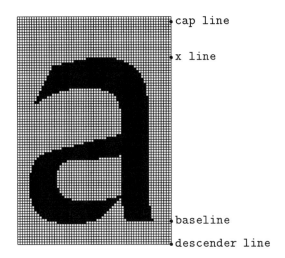

cap line

x line

baseline

descender line

Fig 1. Font character proof made with Metafont; 44% actual size.

4 About Metafont

The original Metafont language was a straightforward realisation by Donald Knuth of his 1977 insight that typeface characters might be drawn 'with *pens* and *parameters* via *programs*' (Knuth 1979, 1985). However, it turned out that many of the features that are necessary in technically satisfactory typeface character shapes were difficult or impossible to draw with the elliptical virtual pens the language used. Examples of such features are flat-bottomed notches at the junctions of descending diagonal strokes, as well as the finials and cutouts that have already been mentioned. The revised version of the language overcame these problems by replacing pen tracks with outlines as its drawing primitive; old Metafont's pens were re-implemented, with greatly extended capabilities, as macros in the new language (Knuth 1986a, 1986b).

Metafont contains its own rasteriser; the output of a program run is a run-length-encoded representation of a set of bitmaps, which can be translated fairly easily into a PostScript Type 3 font. It is possible, though not straightforward, to coerce Metafont into producing outline specifications directly: either by setting an internal switch and editing the resulting log file, or by processing the character programs with Yanai and Berry's *mf2ps* translator (Yanai & Berry 1990).

The emphasis placed by Knuth and his followers on pens as drawing tools, together with his use of them in the Computer

Modern family of typefaces, means that Metafont is generally still seen as a pen-based language. This has tended to obscure the fact that it is also, and indeed primarily, a powerful tool for generating and manipulating character shape specifications based on outlines. Metafont, like PostScript, represents curves as Bézier cubic splines; but outlines in a Metafont program can be handled quite differently from the way they are dealt with in a PostScript font.

The path specifications in a PostScript font are descriptions of character shapes which existed in some form prior to the font's production. 'The character paths must accurately express the true analogue shapes of the original design' (Adobe 1990, ch. 4). The horizontal and vertical hinting mechanisms in the Type 1 font format are ways of preserving, across the hazards of scaling and rasterisation, consistencies that are assumed to be present in the original shapes; they modify, rather than define, the character paths. Metafont, on the other hand, takes consistency as its starting point, and derives its character shapes from the resulting system of constraints. One does not have to subscribe to Knuth's views on the merits of pens as type-drawing tools to recognize the usefulness in a font programming language of named variables with values defined by functions of arbitrary complexity. If there is a dimensional variable called stemwidth whose value is calculated at the beginning of a program run, then every drawing routine that uses it to define the width of a stem will necessarily produce a stroke of the same thickness.

In this respect Metafont's variables closely resemble the entries in TrueType's control value tables. Metafont, though, has no equivalent to TrueType's glyph outline which, like the character paths in a PostScript font, is already defined before the program run begins. Character outlines in Metafont are a consequence of the character programs' execution, rather than a source of information for the programs themselves.

This is not to say, of course, that there are no path specifications in a Metafont character program. Like PostScript, Metafont specifies paths that run between knots, either on the character outline or on the track of a virtual pen. The difference is that in a PostScript font the locations of the knots are specified a priori and once for all in a device-independent character co-ordinate space, while in Metafont they are dynamically specified in device-dependent pixel space by evaluating systems of linear equations.

One consequence of this difference in approach is that fonts produced with Metafont do not necessarily conform to the 'PostScript standard model' in which a single font, with a unique name and a single set of metrics, provides character images over the whole range of output sizes and resolutions. If character shapes are defined in terms of device-dependent units, their widths are likely to be device-dependent as well. In the Computer Modern fonts, Knuth gets around this problem by specifying the character's width in absolute units at the beginning of each character program, and using it as one of the constraints in terms of which the character shape is defined. Our requirement for non-linear scaling meant that Knuth's solution would not work for us. The new fonts consequently required some modifications to USWD's page-makeup software, which had assumed conformity with the PostScript model.

5 Character Drawings

The first drawings that Mandel produced in September 1995 for the USWD typefaces were made on tracing paper over the 89-pixel grid, with stroke-weights specified in pixels and curves drawn in the normal way as continuous lines (Fig. 2). It soon became clear that drawings of this kind, showing character shapes, were not sufficiently informative to serve as originals for a system that could output as proofs the configurations of the character images the fonts it produced would give rise to. Mandel, in drawing character details such as cutouts at junctions and the pointed ends of terminals, was evidently visualising particular configurations of pixels; but it was impossible to tell by looking at the resulting outlines exactly what those configurations were. It was also difficult to reproduce Mandel's corrections, which were made by adding and deleting pixels on the enlarged proofs of font characters, by modifying paths that were specified as curves in the ordinary way.

I therefore suggested to Mandel that he return to a design technique with which he was familiar, and make pixel diagrams (which he called *pre-digitised drawings*) that showed the exact character configurations he wanted (Fig. 3). The weights and widths of the variants in the new typeface family were decided, and the family itself given the name Colorado, at a meeting with

Fig 2. Continuous curve character drawing; 58% actual size. The numbers are pixel counts.

Fig 3. 'Pre-digitised' character drawing; 58% actual size.

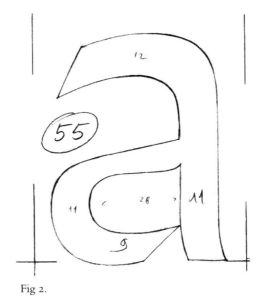

Fig 2.

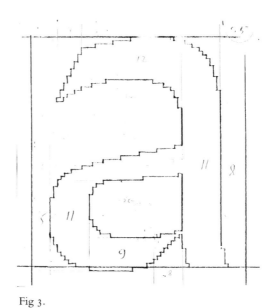

Fig 3.

USWD at Denver in mid-November 1995. By 12 December Mandel had drawn or redrawn almost all the characters for the first variant, the light condensed, in pre-digitised form.

We made the switch from continuous-curve drawings to pixel diagrams because the former did not allow Mandel to define his requirements precisely enough for me to understand them. By their nature, though, the definitions in the diagrams were only fully precise for the nominal character image size that corresponded to the pixel grid on which they were made. Given that USWD needed fonts in a range of sizes, my problem now was to find a way of turning descriptions of pixel configurations into character shape specifications that could be satisfactorily scaled, while retaining the control over image parameters that Mandel demanded.

In my first attempt I adopted a conventional approach, specifying curves by locating tangent points on the pixel grid and controlling curvature by Metafont's tension mechanism. This did not work at all well, mainly because it demanded too many arbitrary choices. Where, for example, is the tangent point of a curve described as a sequence of steps? In effect, as far as curves were concerned, I was trying to turn pixel diagrams back into continuous outlines, introducing inaccuracies as I went. It was clear from the extent of Mandel's corrections to the proofs of the two variants I had produced by the end of May 1996 with this approach that I needed to pay more attention to the pixels as he had drawn them. I therefore devised a way of reproducing the 89-square pixel diagrams exactly, and using the same data to derive character shape specifications that would scale satisfactorily.

This new approach had the immense benefit of making correction a solvable problem. If I could reproduce exactly, in a single pass, every detail of Mandel's changes to the configurations in the 89-pixel fonts, we would not become trapped in the endless loop of modification and correction that the earlier approach had threatened. It also allowed new variants to be built up by modifying the pixel diagrams of earlier ones, with complete confidence that the relationships so created would be preserved in the fonts. Indeed Mandel designed the minuscules of the extra-bold, extra-condensed variant in just this way, by drawing with a felt-tipped pen on the enlarged font-character proofs of the extra-bold condensed.

6 Non-Linear Scaling

Dimensions for the Colorado characters were measured by counting squares on the 89-pixel grid. In the character programs the resulting integer values are held in large arrays indexed by character codes and a style number for each variant. We used the Lumitype convention for style numbering, in which the first digit corresponds to the variant's weight and the second to the reciprocal of its width. Thus, for example, the light condensed, medium normal and extra bold extra condensed have style numbers of 47, 55 and 89 respectively.

Colorado has 93 dimensional parameters in all, almost twice as many as the 48 of the Computer Modern fonts. Because of the differences in our objectives, my approach to parameter scaling differs substantially from Knuth's. His concern was to produce 'a completely precise definition of letter shapes that will produce essentially equivalent results on all raster-based machines' (Knuth 1986b, Preface). Equivalence in this sense, as with the PostScript standard model, is very largely a matter of metrics. The positions of character images should be as nearly as possible identical on pages produced by devices of differing resolutions, and the dimensions of character features should be as nearly identical as the device resolution allows them to be. The values of Computer Modern's dimensional parameters are therefore expressed in device-independent units, and rounded to pixel dimensions only at the moment when a font-making run begins. Also, because he began with a very definite view of the use to which the Computer Modern fonts were intended to be put, Knuth specified a fixed repertory of nominal output sizes, with sets of parameter values explicitly defined for each size. There is nothing in the programs that specifies how to interpolate otherwise than linearly between sizes, or between styles at a given size.[4]

Our objectives for Colorado were quite different. The first priority was to maintain the visual relationships between sets of character images that would be produced in a relatively narrow range of pixel sizes and output resolutions. My target range of pixel sizes was 70-120; in the event, the smallest and largest fonts we used for

4 Knuth's *tour de force* rendering of the 23rd Psalm demonstrates the effects of linear interpolation between the font parameters of old Computer Modern (Knuth 1982).

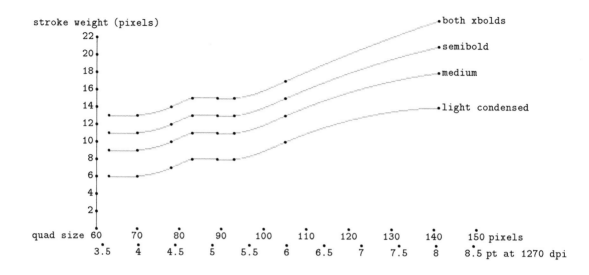

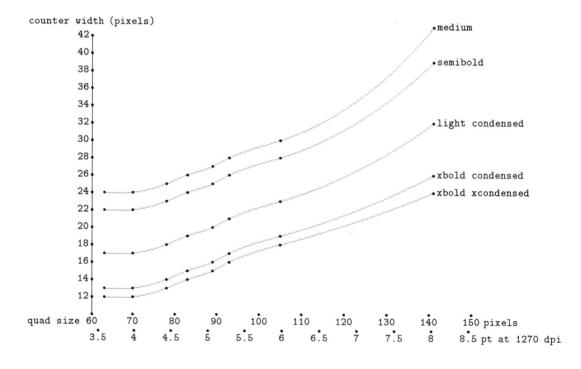

Fig 4. Interpolation curves for stroke-weights and counter widths.

residential directory setting had nominal sizes of 4.5 and 6.0 pt at 1270 dpi, or 79 and 105 pixels respectively. Within the target range we needed to be able to generate sets of fonts at arbitrarily chosen sizes, because we did not know exactly what the typographical requirements of different directory types would be. The legibility of the character images produced by the fonts, as well as the visual differences between them, had to be maintained at every size.

The visual weight of a set of character images depends on their size, stroke-weights, counter widths and side-bearings. Mandel had specified these as pixel counts on his character drawings of the 89-pixel size. I chose the vertical stroke-weight of small n and the counter width of small o as canonical dimensions for each font, and worked out integer values for them by hand, on the basis of scaling and rounding, for key sizes elsewhere within the target range. The resulting vectors were used as data for Hobby's interpolation algorithm (Fig. 4). Other dimensions in the characters were calculated by simple scaling and rounding of their differences from the canonical dimensions.

This technique worked extremely well. Straightforward changes to the values in the interpolation vectors gave us all the control over visual differences that we needed. It was also easily extensible. If it had turned out, for example, that controlling the stroke-weights of capital letters by calculating differences was not satisfactory, an interpolation vector for them could have been set up in just the same way.

Another feature of the Colorado programs allowed us to make limited systematic variations of character weight and width within a font. Vertical and horizontal stroke-weights, vertical distances and horizontal distances are all specified in the programs in terms of different dimensional units. All these units are related to the pixel size of the font, and for simplicity's sake are usually derived from it by identical functions. However, it is not hard to change one function on its own. If the unit in which counter widths are specified, for example, is made larger than the unit used for stroke-weights, characters with counters will become wider without their stroke-weights changing. Curves will conform to the new counter widths, because of the way they are specified. These curves, and the corresponding operation on stroke-weights, provide alternative ways of fine-tuning the visual weight of particular fonts.

AABERG C		
12370 Hummingbird St NW . COON RPDS 55448	**754-0511**	
» Carol J		
10493 Washington Blvd NE .... BLAINE 55434	**757-6267**	
» Dennis G		
12249 Davenport St NE .... BLAINE 55449	**755-2230**	
» G & V 11414 NW Osage St ... COON RPDS 55433	**757-6650**	
» Galen & Barbara		
115 103 Av NW..................... COON RPDS 55448	**757-3171**	
» Steven 17537 NE Swedish Dr . HAM LK 55304	**434-3123**	
AABY Bert C		
16401 Marmoset St NW............. RMSY 55303	**441-4973**	
AAGAARD Robert		
14501 N Diamond Lake Rd .... DAYTON 55327	**421-1096**	
AAKER Stacy		
2811 Cutters Grove Av .... ANOKA 55303	**576-3363**	

AABERG C	
12370 Hummingbird St NW Coon Rpds 55448..	**754-0511**
» Carol J	
10493 Washington Blvd NE Blaine 55434........	**757-6267**
» Dennis G	
12249 Davenport St NE Blaine 55449............	**755-2230**
» G & V 11414 NW Osage St Coon Rpds 55433 ...	**757-6650**
» Galen & Barbara	
115 103 Av NW Coon Rpds 55448	**757-3171**
» Steven 17537 NE Swedish Dr Ham Lk 55304 .	**434-3123**
AABY Bert C	
16401 Marmoset St NW Rmsy 55303...............	**441-4973**
AAGAARD Robert	
14501 N Diamond Lake Rd Dayton 55327	**421-1096**
AAKER Stacy	
2811 Cutters Grove Av Anoka 55303	**576-3363**

Fig 5. Trial settings of residential entries. The type is 5 pt at 1260 dpi, with a baseline separation of 5.5 pt. The data is from the community directory for the northwest suburbs of Minneapolis-Saint Paul.

Mandel was extremely wary of this facility, because he had experienced the bad effects on his designs of anamorphic scaling (which is not quite the same thing). In the event USWD were contractually forbidden to make systematic changes to font parameters that exceeded 5% of their design values.

7 Testing

Because Metafont and TEX are designed to work together, it was very easy to test the fonts with a standard (for the TEX world, at least) set-up of TEX, Tomas Rokicki's *dvips* and a desktop laser printer. Fonts could be made that rendered the 89-pixel characters pixel for pixel at 300 dpi, with a nominal size of 21.4 pt. Proofs composed with these allowed every detail of the character configurations to be checked. Typeset proofs at 1270 dpi were made by uploading the PostScript files produced by *dvips* to Asset Graphics in London, with the output mailed overnight to me at Leckhampstead or within the week to Mandel in France.

In the later stages of the design work we began to feel the need for realistic testing with more extensive material than a few hand-keyboarded entries. USWD sent me 5000-entry extracts from representative examples of their data files; I wrote a TEX header that interpreted the markup in the files. As well as offering a choice of page formats, the header had switches that controlled the formatting of the various entry elements. This allowed us to experiment with different entry styles; particularly with the position and capitalisation of locality names, and the positioning of the postal code before or after the locality (Fig. 5). In later versions the header also provided counts and running averages of the number of entries per page, so that we could evaluate the economic performance of the new typefaces against the existing ones.

8 Conclusion: Font-making as Translation

Was it worth it? In the final accounting, did it make sense to spend so much effort on work that might have been done almost as well and much more quickly by an accomplished operator with Ikarus or Fontographer?

In an earlier paper (Southall 1991) I suggested that in a type manufacturing system there are two principal personalities: the typeface designer and the font producer. The producer's task is to make fonts that give rise to character images whose appearance matches the specifications provided by the designer. Putting this another way, the character images that result from the producer's work should make statements about appearance that are equivalent to the statements made by the objects the designer produces.

In the traditional technique of matrix manufacture for mechanical composition the font producer begins by making character shape specifications in the form of contours. These are realised first as outline drawings, and then as patterns which are mechanically reduced in size to produce the punches from which the matrices are struck (Monotype 1956).

These contour-defined objects cannot speak of appearance in the same way that character images do. For one thing they are normally much larger, and the appearance of an object changes with its size. For another, they are defined by boundaries of a different kind. The drawings and patterns have *shapes*, bounded by smooth curves. Character images, whether produced by photography, xerography or ink transfer, have *configurations*, but they do not have shapes in the same sense that outline drawings do. It is only in exceptional circumstances that the boundary of a character image is smooth enough to allow a contour-defined shape to be derived from it without a great deal of abstraction. It is instructive to contrast Gonczarowski's expectation that images for auto-tracing will be around 2500 pixels square (Gonczarowski 1991) with typical digitally-typeset characters in text, which even at high resolutions are normally no more than a fifth of that size.

Part of the font producer's skill in the traditional technique was a mental ability to translate the shapes of large contour-defined objects into the appearance of the smaller configurationally defined images they would give rise to. Designers who were at ease with the production process shared the same skill. 'Personal experience has shown that given the opportunity to compare the large letter drawings with proofs of the characters at actual type size it is possible, after a time, to develop fairly reliable judgement as to what will be the final effect of a letter that is drawn many times larger than life' (Tracy 1986, ch. 16). But in that technique the marking process that produced the character images had little influence on the images' metric characteristics. Inking and impression do not alter the underlying proportions of the letter on the face of a type.

In what we may call the classical technique of digital font-making (Stone 1991), the font producer still translates from the designer's appearance specifications to the shape specifications of a contour-defined intermediate. This uses, if designer and producer are the same person and the contours are specified directly, the same skill that Tracy speaks of. However, in normal practice it is the rasteriser that translates from the intermediate's shape to the image's configuration; and, as was shown in Section 3 above, at small pixel sizes a rasteriser working in unmodified character co-ordinate space necessarily mistranslates the metric characteristics of the design in certain circumstances. Because he sets such store by the relationships between the weights and proportions of the variants in his typeface families, it was these mistranslations that Mandel complained of in his strictures on the performance of PostScript fonts. Type 1 stroke-weight hinting is no help here; all it can do is to make sure that the rasteriser mistranslates consistently.

I originally asked Mandel for pre-digitised drawings because, in my role as font producer, I could not translate faithfully enough from the shape language of the outlines he had provided into the appearance language of the character configurations he had in mind. In making the new drawings, though, Mandel hoped for an opportunity to short-circuit the translation process altogether, speaking directly of image appearance in terms of image configuration as he had with his designs for CRT photo-composing machines. Making Type 3 bitmaps from the drawings would have allowed him to do this, but did not meet USWD's requirements.

Given that some translation had to be done, the question was which tool to use. In working with Metafont rather than making Type 1 fonts I was effectively building my own translation robot, rather than using the one supplied with PostScript's font machinery.

The PostScript robot, though fast and reliable, was limited; it read only contours as source texts, and translated only into configurations. Also, its covers were sealed and plainly marked *No User-Serviceable Parts Inside*. My machine was more versatile, in that it could reproduce or paraphrase a configuration source text as well as translating a contour one (and indeed would, under protest, do configuration-to-contour translations and contour-to-contour paraphrases as well, as I suggest in Section 4 above). All its covers were removable; parts sometimes fell out.

Robots get built, generally speaking, to provide solutions to problems that for one reason or another cannot be solved in any other way - or for which the builder does not know of another solution. In the Colorado project, font-making with Metafont made three things possible that, in the context of the time, seemed hard or impossible to achieve by any other means. These were, in order of their occurence in the project, allowing Mandel to express his wishes exactly in the form of pre-digitized drawings; solving the consequent correction problem, and thus giving him confidence in the technique's validity; and, last and most important, providing us with precise control of the visual relationships between typeface variants over the whole range of directory formats. Without these, the project could not have succeeded as it has so far.

9 Acknowledgements

To Bob Callison of USWD for co-ordinating the Colorado project with endless patience and good humour, and to his staff in Denver and Omaha for their undaunted enthusiasm in dealing with out-of-the-way features of the Metafont system. Also to Beat Stamm of Microsoft, for opening my eyes at ATypI'97 to what I might have been able to do with TrueType.

References

Adobe Systems, Inc. *Adobe Type 1 font format*. Reading (Mass.): Addison-Wesley, 1990

Carter, H. G. 'Optical scale in typefounding.' *Typography* **4** 2–6 (1937)

Gonczarowski, J. 'A fast approach to auto-tracing (with parametric cubics).' In Morris, Robert A. & Jacques André (eds.),

Raster imaging and digital typography II. Cambridge: Cambridge University Press, 1991

Knuth, D. E. *TEX and Metafont: new directions in typesetting*. Bedford (Mass.): Digital, 1979

Knuth, D. E. 'The concept of a meta-font'. *Visible Language* **16** (1) 3–27 (1982)

Knuth, D. E. 'Lessons learned from Metafont'. *Visible Language* **19** (1) 35–53 (1985)

Knuth, D. E., *Computer Modern typefaces*. Reading (Mass.): Addison-Wesley, 1986

Knuth, D. E. *The METAFONTbook*. Reading (Mass.): Addison-Wesley, 1986

Mandel, L 'Il nuovo carattere Galfra per gli elenchi telefonici italiani.' *Graphicus* **9** (1978)

Monotype Corporation. '"Monotype" matrices and moulds in the making'. *Monotype Recorder* **40** (1) (1956)

Seybold, J. W. *The world of digital typesetting*. Media (Pennsylvania): Seybold Publications, 1984

Southall, R. *Designing new typefaces with Metafont* (Report STAN-CS-85-1074). Stanford University: Department of Computer Science, 1985

Southall, R. 'Designing a new typeface with Metafont.' In Desarmenien, J. (ed.), *TEX for scientific documentation*. Berlin: Springer, 1986

Southall, R. 'Character description techniques in type manufacture.' In Morris, Robert A. & Jacques André (eds.), *Raster imaging and digital typography II*. Cambridge: Cambridge University Press, 1991

Stone, S. *On Stone: the art and use of typography on the personal computer*. San Francisco: Bedford Arts, 1991

Tracy, Walter. *Letters of credit: a view of type design*. London: Gordon Fraser, 1986

Yanai, S. & Berry, D. M. 'Environment for translating Metafont to PostScript.' *TUGboat* **11** (4) 525–541 (1990)

PART 5

TYPOGRAPHY AND EDUCATIONAL SOFTWARE

The design of educational software

ROSEMARY SASSOON LETTERFORM CONSULTANT, WRITER AND RESEARCHER sassoon@centrenet.co.uk

Letterforms are only one of the typographic factors to be considered. Trying to educate educators or software designers of the necessity to consider other elements that would improve educational software has proven difficult.

Learning by design: the role of design in facilitating learning

ROGER DICKINSON, DIRECTOR OF THE CENTRE FOR LEARNING TECHNOLOGY, FACULTY OF SCIENCE, UNIVERSITY OF WESTERN AUSTRALIA roger@uniwa.uwa.edu.au

This chapter offers a developer's view of how the design of multimedia programme may influence learning. The term multimedia has been taken to encompass interactive computer software programs specifically developed as learning resources.

ROSEMARY SASSOON

The design of educational software

This chapter starts with a progress report of the Sassoon family of child orientated typefaces. From a researched beginning the family has been influenced by market forces and helped by an advance of technology that enabled my concept of variability and flexibility within any set of letters to be accomplished at reasonable cost. With the development of internet marketing, it has become possible to reach specialised users directly, free from the inflexibility of traditional type vendors. This in itself makes an interesting study. Then a more intractable problem is discussed: how to persuade software manufacturers to consider other typographic and design factors that might make their wares more educationally effective and more user-friendly.

In the previous volume of *Computers and Typography* I reported the research that led to the design of child orientated typefaces. In the intervening years this project has flourished and spread around the world from its modest beginning. First envisaged for use in books, it had another, somewhat different objective: to pinpoint

When you travel ...

Our global travel network gives absolute confidence, with accurate, reliable and up-to-the-minute travel information only a phone call away.

You never can tell how your typefaces are going to be used. These examples are both from Japanese advertisements, one from a travel firm the other from a car manufacturer.

The gripping new All-Wheel Drive Subaru Liberty Sedan.

a b c d e f g h i j k l m n o

G g
Gåter

From a Norwegian
ABC by Soria Moria,
published by Det
Norske Samlaget

Kan du gjette gåter?

 Hva er det i grøt-gryta
som verken grisen eller hunden vil ha?

 Hva er det som går bort til alle hus,
men aldri kommer inn?

 Oransje på kroppen og grønn i toppen.
Hvem er jeg?

 Hva gjør en glassmester
når det ikke er noe glass igjen?

the need to consider children's own preferences instead of imposing adult views, recommended by adult experts, on young readers. As the use of computers in schools grew, so did the need for such typefaces that would be legible on screen. At the same time the technology for designing typefaces became cheaper and easier to manage. It became possible to be more flexible in the way our family of fonts worked in allowing choice of alternative letterforms, for instance, without incurring vast expense. We have personalised the original Primary forms for various clients without sacrificing the original concept of clarity and child friendliness. A good example is the Montessori font which has rounded baseline terminals to enable the production of large sandpaper letters that would not feel too sharp for small fingers. By allowing form to follow function, a subtly different typeface emerged. This latest addition has been a set of three progressive joined up fonts with the necessary built-in flexibility to satisfy my views on joined scripts for teaching handwriting. Like the other fonts, these will quite likely be used for advertising and other purposes that were not originally envisaged.

Legibility tests

From the moment the first font was designed it became inappropriate for me to undertake research into the effectiveness of my own designs. This had to be left to others. All further developments were to meet needs of the market – the market being both publishers and educationists. There is no empirical proof that these newer fonts are more effective than any other. All we can say is that they seem to work. There are many problems when it comes to assessing legibility and proclaiming definite findings about many of the aspects of typefaces, especially where children are concerned. Legibility is not an absolute. It is subject to many variables and there is little that you can take for granted. You might think, for instance, that what a child is accustomed to they would read most easily, but there are always those who choose the unfamiliar for whatever reason. You will only find out why by questioning the child. I have seen student projects that worked on this principle and reported valuable findings. Unfortunately, such research is sometimes perceived as a relatively simple job. One particular project was recently given to a researcher who seemed to know nothing about typography. It used a small sample of readers and muddled point sizes so that, visually, some examples appeared to be considerably smaller than others. Not surprisingly the larger letters and resulting longer line lengths were perceived as easier to read, destroying any hope of a fair comparison of the typefaces involved and completely distorting the findings. Even so it was published in a reputable journal where it could, if taken seriously, be detrimental to those it was meant to help.

We need to be more honest in our expectations and more searching in our methodology if we are to get near to the truth in such a complex area. We may need to have quite different ways of testing. When Professor Arnold Wilkins (then at the Medical Research Council Applied Psychology Unit, Cambridge) was considering some tests with children involving various aspects of typefaces and visual effects, we discussed different methods of testing legibility. Tests originally devised for adults seemed inappropriate for children. Most tests currently in use consist of reading a passage and judging speed, accuracy and expressiveness. Classes are likely to consist of children of mixed ability, some of whom may not be fluent readers. I had felt for a long time that elements that might confuse reading speed with comprehension should be removed from a test that is solely to assess legibility. If random, simple words were used this should result in a more accurate findings. I took no further part in formulating *The Rate of Reading Test*, as it came to be known, but that was how it all began. The Pilot version was published in 1994 (A J Wilkins, R J Jeanes, P D Pumfrey, M Lasker & R Sassoon). The procedure was described this way: 'Subjects are required to read text that looks like a passage of prose, but consists of random words. The reading is independent of syntactic and semantic constraints but requires all the usual visual and visuo-perceptual processing.'

Hughes and Wilkins (2000) provide a useful survey of research into typograpy in children's books. They describe the test this way, after agreeing that speed and accuracy are both important: 'The Rate of Reading test differs from conventional reading tests that are designed to assess scholastic attainment in reading and compare one individual's performance with that of another. It is designed to compare each participant's performance under different visual conditions: reading speeds vary considerably from person to person.' To my knowledge this test has not been used to look at reading from the screen, but would be ideally suited for that purpose

The marketing of child-orientated typefaces
The increased use of computers in education has not only affected the spread of the Sassoon typefaces but the method of marketing them. The traditional way of allowing typefounders to market newly designed fonts has proved too inflexible because it would

not reach those who would not normally know where to find such products. Companies such as Linotype, Adobe and Monotype have done a reasonable job of getting our typefaces to designers and publishers around the world, but educationists have little contact with them. The traditional type vendors were too inflexible to reach them. It was by licensing directly to hardware manufacturers who supplied schools that our major breakthrough was made. This was only after educating them about the need for legible child-orientated typefaces (and the add-on value and advertising opportunities for their products). Teachers are understandably wary of advertising material, and at first we allowed our work to spread by word of mouth and personal recommendation. This was awkward for some people but eventually they found us. At least we avoided the reputation of overemphasising the virtues of our product.

The website

There is a right time for each stage of marketing. It would have been pointless to have a website before our customers had sufficient knowledge or equipment to find it. Designing it so that inexperienced users could make the requisite choices to place an order was a typographic exercise in itself, as Adrian Williams explains: 'Website design is still a new medium. In the few years since its rise, all those who specialise in design have had to balance their wish to impose their ideas with a rigid and slowly changing text programming language that is HTML. Many lose the battle and end with a hotch potch of clever design elements with little direction for the web surfer.

   'Simpler pages are the key to easy navigation of the site. Not all clever design elements can be seen in all web browsers anyway. We have distinct panels of text which link to the information. No clever widgets, just solid information. We don't accept credit card payments, so the surfer relies on an Order Form to confirm prices of items when sending the email message. The vast majority of order forms are correct. Getting it right first time when addressing what is essentially a world audience is an impossible goal for the web designer. There are always a few who are so new to the technology that they need help. In these cases we take note of their problems and modify the website accordingly, as all good sites should.'

Starter fonts Pack of 4 fonts for Parents/Teachers teaching infants to read and write...

Infant, Medium, Tracker, Dotted

Primary Educational fonts that accentuate word shape for early reading and writing

Typefaces bridging the gap between reading and writing for children

Maximum legibility for many adult, multimedia and screen uses

Fonts providing maximum legibility for adults. Particularly useful on computer screens

Sans

Italic 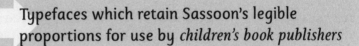 *Designed for use with any Sassoon family for emphasis (not a handwriting model)*

Book Typefaces which retain Sassoon's legible proportions for use by *children's book publishers*

Sassoon® Montessori Fonts specially designed for handwriting exercises

Sassoon®Joiner *Software application to 'join' Sassoon. Create your own handwriting scheme!*

The CD

Several years ago Apple UK attempted to introduce the typefaces to educational users on a CD, but it proved unsuccessful because the schools were not all equipped and certainly not yet ready to make their purchases in this way. After some ten years in operation, now with some 15 typefaces and numerous choices to make we have had to reconsider our method of marketing. Adrian Williams explains: 'Floppy disks have been the transfer media of choice for many years. Even when there was too much to fit on one diskette, special applications were conceived to compress and then rejoin files together on the users Hard Disk. Floppy drives are no longer fitted in computers as a matter of course. Various media storage devices are competing for inclusion in the Desktop computers we buy. The Compact Disk has been the most successful.

'Now, all computers arrive with CD capability. The computer's own software arrives on a CD because the files are so huge. With users so familiar with the media and the availability of CD writers and the disks at an affordable price, it was the obvious choice when offering the whole range of Sassoon typefaces.

'We created an interface that looks the same on both Windows and MacOS systems. Then we built it into an application on a free CD along with all of the fonts 'locked' in an encrypted file. Now when we get enquiries, the CD copes with everything. There are essentially three sections. A Browser panel lets the user look at basic samples of the typefaces and to make a selection of the ones of interest.

'The Order panel enables a form to be printed with automatically calculated prices for faxing or posting with a payment. When we receive the order an 'unlocking code' is sent to enable the user to unlock the font items from the CD. Inevitably there are bugs in the software which are fixed as soon as we are made aware of them. Coupled with the website and free technical support to help users through the first five minutes of use, we have found the whole enterprise a rewarding and easier method of marketing. Eventually, when payment by credit card becomes a more secure transaction, we hope to include this in our service along with the continuing development of the whole site and the products it offers.'

Other factors to consider

Letterforms are only one of the typographic design factors to be considered. Trying to educate educators or software manufacturers of the necessity to consider other elements that would improve educational software has proven far more difficult. While huge investment in expensive hardware goes ahead relentlessly, the efficacy of educational software goes virtually unquestioned. The content may be assessed for its teaching potential, but whether learning could be more effective if the typographic approach were more professionally directed is still ignored. Several years ago I was given a small grant by national organisation (which had better remain nameless considering what I am going to say) to produce flexible, simple guidelines for software manufacturers.

My starting point was to contact the manufacturers themselves. It seemed logical to ascertain what type of guidelines they provided for their technological staff. It transpired that only one major company had ever issued any design guidelines at all. Those, however, had been lost and no one could remember what instructions had been included.

The next stage was to consult people in different disciplines for their views. The first remark came from an IT advisor: 'I am constantly asked to recommend educational software that looks like a computer game.' This goes straight to perhaps the most fundamental point: should educational software resemble a computer game or should its visual language signal that it is primarily for learning? Should it not project a quieter more serious aspect that might improve the environment for learning? Exceptions could be made for reluctant learners or special needs.

The next comment came from an advisory teacher who stressed that she did not agree with it: 'It is perceived wisdom that children learn in a different way today – in the whizz-bang society.' Do children really learn in a different way, or has this been adults' perception, carefully manipulated by the software industry? It could be an assumption based on children's obvious enjoyment of computer games and the novelty of the technology. But it is only an assumption and the reverse may be just as true: that children retain little in permanent memory from game-like techniques, and the techniques learned in such games do not transfer specifically into other skills. It is probably true that the rising generation of students have been computer literate since infancy, and most likely can tolerate a far busier screen than their parents. Toleration is one thing, but whether they would function better with less distraction is another point.

'Most educational software is gaudy and tawdry and I am unwilling to have it in my school', said one headmaster. 'Options fighting for space only cause confusion' and 'Avoid flickering and dazzle and anything with flashing lights' were two more observations. 'Box only short sentences or phrases, then smaller type with plenty of space around it can be absorbed at a glance' was the comment of an informed teacher.

These and other remarks gave me some hope that educationists, who after all are the purchasers of such software, would be able to exert pressure on manufacturers to pay more attention to the presentation of their products – but this level of knowledge was soon found to be unusual.

Before I had time to complete my report I was summoned to address a group of some 50 IT advisory teachers. When I tried to explain the kind of guidelines I proposed and what teachers might do to influence the situation, the response was far from positive. 'We do not even know how to lay out a worksheet effectively, so how can we be expected to make the judgements that you are suggesting?' was the reply. That worksheets are badly laid out is certainly true, that educational books are also poorly designed and do not work as good examples is also true. Layout and design are taught skills; they are not natural to many of us. Few people in education recognise their importance. Today teachers have the responsibility of producing pupil material and are given expensive equipment capable of producing a professional standard of printing, but often lack the skill even to see what they are doing wrong. They deserve having the basics of this skill introduced into initial or in-service teacher training.

The guidelines

So what were these guidelines that so worried the IT teachers? They were so simple and flexible that I would say they were just common sense. To begin with, the precise purpose of the software must be considered. Here are a few categories of the many that might require different typographic consideration:

a For developing discriminatory skills at an early age
b For developing coordination
c For teaching sequential skills
d For encouraging creative writing
e For allowing children to access encyclopaedic knowledge
f To support the teaching of factual subjects, in particular scientific or technological subjects involving many diagrams
g For foreign language teaching

At every age and stage such software might be divided into that which is to introduce new material and that which is to reinforce a previously taught skill. At every level the typographic and design criteria might differ.

Some differences between the screen and the printed page
It is a reasonable assumption that children know that the conventional place to commence reading a printed page is at the top left of any body of text. There is by no means such certainty with many complex screen displays. Where to begin and in which order to assimilate and use the information needs to be signalled by the layout. The assumption that the heaviest type would stress the most important issue or starting point is no longer necessarily valid. It is quite likely that on a busy screen the spacial factors would affect where the eye would first alight and so determine the sequence of attention. Whatever technique is employed only a few points can be stressed, so the important ones must be selected first and the layout built around them.

How information should be laid out for the printed page and for adult readers has been researched and endlessly discussed over the centuries. Even this information, not entirely relevant to the subject under discussion, is largely ignored by those who seem to think that just by using a DTP program decisions get made somehow by the computer. A computer cannot make aesthetic or ergonomic decisions. In educational software it often seems that by using the latest complex graphic techniques, designers (perhaps encouraged by the marketing department) think they are projecting an expert or expensive atmosphere in their products. Maybe they are right and this does impress the uninformed purchaser, often to the disadvantage of the users. Without considering the possible detrimental effect on children's eyes, it must be understood that the layout of any document or screen will affect how easily the information in it will be assimilated.

Some general issues

1 Keep the screen simple and well organised.
2 Navigational aids need to be clear and easily understood, likewise control keys and tools. It helps if they appear in the same position throughout a whole range of software
3 Icons, for whatever purpose, need to be carefully designed to suit that purpose, and the age, stage and perhaps culture of the intended user. What may appear attractive to designers may not be comprehensible to young users.
4 Spacing is even more important on screen than on paper. Each item, whether text or illustration should be compact within its own space, and separated by adequate space from the next one. It is quite likely that the message with the most space around it will be the first to attract the child's attention on a screen with several blocks of text and illustrations. Captions should be positioned carefully so that they are instantly assimilated along with the relevant illustration. When positioning text within boxes it is not the size or weight of the letters that counts so much as the margin of space around the text in the box. In some cases the letters of messages can be seen to touch the outline of the box, a situation made even worse if the box is filled with colour. Avoid justified text, especially when there are short lines of text, however desirable this may appear from the designer's point of view. Justification disrupts word spacing and can distract and confuse young readers. A slightly different spacing issue concerns interactive programs: make sure that there is sufficient space for children to put in their replies.
5 Colour and contrast are issues that need careful consideration, not only from the point of view of how a child assimilates knowledge, but in relation to the dazzle and fatigue they may impose on the eye. Too many colours splashed across the screen will distract the viewer and dissipate their concentration. Care should be taken with the choice and contrast of colours and how they are used together on the screen. One colour imposed on top of another needs even more care. Colour on top of

colour on top of another colour and even outlined in a fourth can be found. Far from helping the user this will obscure the message. Subtle colours that blend are more restful than those which contrast blatantly. Tonal contrasts may be just as effective. Short messages can sometimes be shown white (intaglio) through a coloured panel. For older pupils who need to memorise the content, it is better that colour, particularly when illustrations are involved, should not extend behind and impinge on the text.

6 Dazzle, whether caused by colour, brightness, contrast, certain patterns of text or screen flicker, may distract the viewer. It may tire them or give them a headache. It can affect some children more seriously. See Wilkins (1995) *Visual Discomfort* for more on this complex subject.

7 Illustrations are vital in many cases but they should be used to add to the learning process and not merely as decoration, when they become a distraction. Areas of illustration relating to different subjects or activities should be well separated from each other and should usually be kept clear of text. Many activity templates appear too visually busy. Almost all would profit from better sizing, spacing and fewer and less luridly coloured illustrations. Many screen layouts give the impression that the illustrators have been given the freedom to splash as many extraneous pictures as possible around so as to justify their fee. Little thought has been given to how this haphazard use of illustration and allied colour might affect the task that is supposed to be being taught to the child.

8 Legibility in the classroom is, in some ways, trickier to achieve on screen than in a book. It is certainly different. There is a need for fast word recognition for children who may not be competent readers. To complicate matters, there may be shared activities where not all participants will be at the optimum distance from the screen. Some of the issues related to letterforms that may need addressing are the choice and weight of typeface, word and line spacing, line length and the use of boxing or underlining of text. To achieve optimum word recognition the fashionable shortening of ascenders and descenders must be addressed. These letterforms have come about because of the desirability of fitting as much information

as possible into a limited space, such as in newspapers, where it is assumed that the readers are fluent. Even if legibility is considered, it is only ascenders that are lengthened, because research (with adults) has shown that readers only need to scan the top half of a word to recognise it. It is not so with children, and for no age group is there the same necessity to cram as much text as possible on to a screen. It may be supposed that typefaces with adequate ascenders and descenders take up more space, but it can be shown that even with slightly smaller body size to compensate, they can still help to make text clearer to read. Boxing of words or phrases on the screen flattens the visual appearance of letters, making longer ascenders and descenders even more helpful in accentuating the word shape.

It is a mistaken concept that bold type is always easier to read. It is often quite the opposite. By emboldening letters the recognition points may become distorted. This applies equally to icons that have been made bolder than originally designed. Several lines of bold text can create a pattern that is both dazzling and potentially dangerous to some who are inclined to visual disturbances or migraine.

There is another mistaken concept about what constitutes easier reading. That concerns capital letters. Their lack of height differentials make them less, not more, easily recognisable. They should be used only in headlines, and then sparingly. Contrast and emphasis can be achieved with sizing or other techniques, such as the use of a light tint behind a body of text.

Conclusions

There are many more details that could have been included, but the report was meant primarily as an awareness-raising exercise. My enquiries had already revealed that most of those involved in producing educational software were not aware of the factors raised here. Even employing a 'designer' would not help much unless they were all aware of the specialised nature of this field. The whole emphasis of the training of graphic designers seems to have altered in recent years. Students are encouraged to impress their own style and personality on the task, which may be the right policy in some jobs. The old fashioned dictum: 'Follow your brief even if it blows out of the window' is seen as just that – old-fashioned. Anyhow, in the situation under discussion, it is unlikely that anyone would be qualified to issue a detailed brief or ensure that the designer kept to it. Discussions with several design departments revealed that it was very unlikely their graduates would be aware of the special requirements of educational software. My recommendation was that such an enterprise needs a multi-disciplinary team working together and learning from testing their products in the classroom. Such a group might consist of technician, specialist teacher, program writer (in the creative sense), experienced graphic designer and perhaps a marketing person. Above all there should be a team leader whose job it would be to ensure that the interests of one member of the group should not override those of the rest – especially the interests of children.

I had neither time nor resources to translate these guidelines into research. Anyhow, you can research and produce guidelines but the real problem remains how to persuade an industry to pay any attention when they can see no profit in spending money on the expertise needed to follow them. By the time my report was completed those who had commissioned it had moved on. Their successors informed me that they were not considering publishing it or, as far as I know, even circulating it informally. I think that is indicative of how little importance was given to this subject even by those who should be safeguarding children's interests.

It was with some relief that I heard of the work that had been undertaken by the Development Unit for Instructional Technology in the Department of Human Movement at the University of Western Australia (now The Centre for Learning Technology). They have the resources and skill to carry out extensive research. Their software shows just what can be produced by researching the effect of layout and design on the learning process. They put into practice the clear guidelines that they evolved along with the techniques that they have developed through testing and re-testing with appropriately aged pupils. It is a great pleasure to have this important work reported here.

References

Hughes L E and Wilkins A J (2000) *Typography in Children's Reading Schemes*. Journal of Research in Reading.
Wilkins A J (1995) *Visual Discomfort*. Oxford University Press.

ROGER DICKINSON

Learning by Design: The role of design in facilitating learning

Instructional Design

The evolution of the book has left us with a medium of breath-taking simplicity and power. Its conventions are well established, a large body of expertise exists to guide the design of each different element from content to layout to cover, and the different forms of the genre are clearly understood by both creators and consumers. By comparison, the computer, as a medium for delivering learning material, is not yet at all well understood.

In establishing a new technology, we commonly adopt the known conventions of an existing technology. The bodies of the first horseless carriages looked like coaches, the wheels like carriage wheels, and the lights like coach lamps. There was no consensus as to the function of the different controls. Gradually, as the genre became better understood, designers developed new conventions, and their acceptance facilitated a greater exploitation of the potential of the technology. So it comes as no surprise that the early days of multimedia have seen a rash of metaphors and techniques that mimic the conventions of print-pages, indexes, folders, cards, notebooks and so on. Developers adopt widely divergent approaches, and users exhibit a variety of expectations. Happily, like the early adopters of the motorcar, we can look forward to the emergence of greater consistency in form and function.

This evolution will be critical in the drive to develop effective and appealing electronic learning materials. This chapter offers an developer's view of how the design of a multimedia program may influence learning. Throughout the chapter, the term "multimedia" has been taken to encompass interactive computer software programs specifically developed as learning resources. The vast scale of the internet offers the ultimate in open-ended exploration, but this magnifies the risks of disorientation and fruitless exploration, and reduces the opportunities for teachers and designers to structure the learning experience. This chapter focuses upon the confined multimedia environments delivered via CD ROMs, Intranets and Managed Learning Environments, where the instructional designer has control over the material offered to the learner. Many lessons can be drawn from this for the effective design of on-line materials.

The illustrations are drawn from programs developed by DUIT Multimedia at The University of Western Australia.

How And Why We Learn

Learning is an individual activity that is most effective when learners are able to draw their own conclusions from the experience. Learners need the time, space and opportunity for individual thought and study to test their learning and satisfy themselves about what they have learned. Interaction is important to the learning process to enable the learner to test their understanding against the views of others.

An effective learning program will encourage a deep, rather than a superficial, approach to learning, promoting an active relationship with the material. It should relate previous knowledge and personal experience to the task, and relate evidence to conclusions. The material must engage the learner's interest, offer variety, connect with prior learning, offer opportunities to choose content and study methods, supply clear goals, and have the learner's needs at heart.

Many forms of instruction require that the learner adapt to the instruction. Effectively designed multimedia can accommodate a variety of individual differences, including cognitive style, by delivering information in contextually meaningful sequences, at a variable pace controlled by the learner, and by engaging several of the senses.

The design of learning material (*instructional design*) and its presentation (*interface design*) can play an important part in achieving many of these goals, and an appreciation of how and why we learn should underpin all multimedia design.

Learners create knowledge by building connections between their existing knowledge and new information. The software must allow and encourage the learner to make these connections. From an affective point of view it is important that users of multimedia programs feel that they are in control of their learning and of the pace with which they proceed through the information. Exercising that control promotes feelings of competence, a sense of relevance and motivation.

Readiness for learning is an indicator of motivation and a desire to learn. To be intrinsically motivating, multimedia material must be informative, stimulate curiosity, meet the needs of the users, "speak the user's language", promote feelings of competence and self-efficacy, and offer a degree of challenge. The potential outcomes of the activity and the knowledge and skills to be gained should be made clear to the learner so that they can assess the personal value of the learning activity.

The design should match the characteristics of the learners – who they are, their entry skills and knowledge, their cultural background, ages and gender, and their level of computer literacy. The content may need to be multilingual or include different

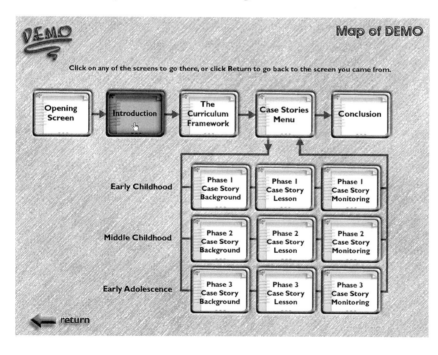

Figure 1. Maps not only provide the user with a mental image of the program structure, but can be used to navigate through the material.

versions of the same language (for example, English and American spelling). Different users will have different degrees of prior cultural knowledge of the content. An awareness of multicultural and gender issues is an important design consideration, and thought must be given to the cultural messages being projected in the material to ensure that they are not distracting or unpalatable.

Structure & content

Multimedia programs may have complex hierarchical structures that provide learners with too many choices, leading to confusion and disorientation, and this makes it difficult to build effective connections between an existing knowledge structure and new information. To encourage familiarity and confidence, the structure of multimedia learning materials should be logical, apparent and accessible, and learners should be provided with the tools to help orientate themselves within the structure, such as maps revealing the overall layout. (*Figure 1*).

Research has indicated that instruction should follow a logical sequence based upon the needs of the learner, and that path and pace should not be left totally at the learner's discretion. An effective instructional design technique is to structure the material in a linear and hierarchical mix, and provide the navigation tools to exploit both structures. Novices who lack the confidence to blaze their own trails begin by following an explicit linear path prepared by the content expert. As confidence rises, learners begin to act more spontaneously, moving away from the laid-down path and following up points of interest.

The structure and function of multimedia programs lend themselves very readily to the concept of *sequencing*. Content may be sequenced by gathering like-concepts together and by confining the amount of information on each screen *(Figure 2)*. The sequencing of information should allow for different cognitive styles, and for the fact that learners can only process a certain amount of information in a given period. To challenge gifted students, as well as provide remediation to novices, an effective design will provide instruction at different levels of difficulty.

Users view a multimedia program through a rectangular window (the screen) that limits the amount of information they can view. In a sense this isolates that chunk of material from any that has

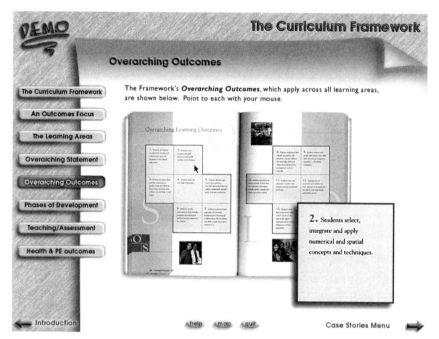

Figure 2. This screen brings together eight related layers of information, accessed via the left-hand column of buttons.

been viewed previously or is yet to come. To make matters worse, learners can often move through screens of information in any order they choose. For this, and other reasons, a certain amount of *redundancy* appears to be important in the content and structure of a multimedia program. (Redundancy is a measure of the inherent order in a system. A typical English language text is often 50% redundant.) Concepts may need to be mentioned several times. A glossary that can be accessed by the learner from any point in the program (typically by clicking on a word or phrase) offers obvious benefits.

Knowledge should not be articulated to the learner. Multimedia in confined environments (disk-based, Intranets and Managed Learning Environments) can offer an effective degree of *guided discovery learning*. By structuring the content to enhance a climate of discovery, learners can be encouraged to make links between their existing knowledge and new information, and to uncover relationships for themselves before their findings are confirmed and explained. Simulations and problem-based learning are very effective in this regard.

The book is a wonderful medium for the delivery of text and

illustrations: a more complex technology like multimedia should only be used when it adds value, especially when it is disk-based. (Value takes many forms, including dynamic elements such as audio, video, animation, QuickTime Virtual Reality objects and panoramas, simulations, interaction, multiple paths, etc.) With current screen technology, text is much better suited to print technology. Even on the Web (where distribution advantages may override a print-based alternative) it is disappointing to see so many multimedia programs that offer nothing more than text and illustrations.

Multimedia is inherently a visual and spatial medium. Concepts can be rendered graphically, linked to others and systematically laid out on the screen as a set of ideas. The inclusion of value-adding media can enhance the clarity of the concepts being presented, reflecting an awareness of different cognitive styles and extending the richness of the information being presented. Researchers have suggested that the multiplicity of sensory media available can be used significantly for critical educational effect. Some things are better learned through dynamic visual and acoustic media, especially if they are user-controlled, and many individuals learn better from more sensory media.

The incorporation of moving images and audio opens up many different instructional design possibilities. The ability to control time-based phenomena is a critical aspect of understanding them. By using audio and video controls a learner can move at will through clips, controlling the pace, switching between views and re-examining critical points *(Figure 3)*.

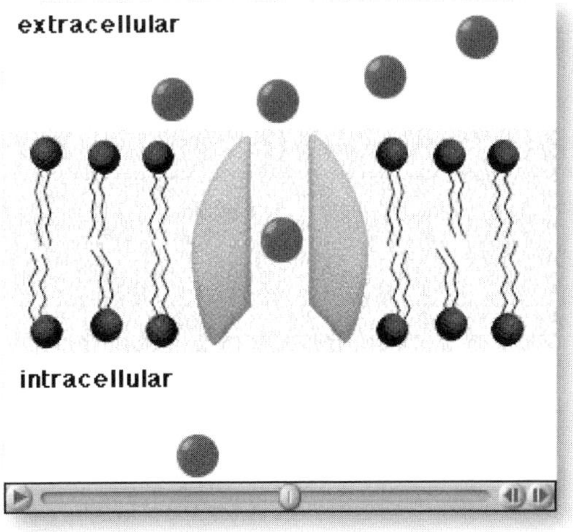

There is little empirical evidence concerning the merits of *colour* in a multimedia program, although it has been generally held that the use of multiple colour fonts will reduce legibility. That aside, we live in a multi-coloured world and interface designers should exploit the motivational and attention-getting features of colour to enhance the presentation of information. Learning and retention may well be more effective when learners

Figure 3. The video bar below the image gives the user control over a complex animated sequence.

enjoy their visual interaction with the material.

Boundaries are imposed in the early stages of all new technologies. Although disk-based multimedia is now capable of high-fidelity audio, desktop video has not yet achieved television quality (without additional hardware). Web-based multimedia has severe limitations on audio and video quality. These are transient compromises that will steadily become unnecessary. Designers may have to acknowledge existing technical limitations, but should not let them become an excuse for poor quality. Screen technology offers very high standards of colour and image fidelity, and today's learners have a right to expect the same professional presentation standards in their learning programs as they encounter in current computer games, television and films.

Interaction

An active involvement in learning is far more effective than passive learning. Multimedia's most important quality, and the factor that distinguishes it from other learning technologies, is its capacity for meaningful *interaction*, and instructional designers should facilitate this at every opportunity. Unlike many other educational media (such as videotapes and broadcast television) and other educational methods (such as lectures or audio tutorials), control of the exploration of a multimedia program is vested in the learner.

Interaction can take many forms. Simply operating the program involves the learner, especially where this involves something more than merely clicking the "Next Screen" control. Exploring video sequences by moving back and forth through the clip can build a better understanding of a dynamic event.

Simulations offer opportunities for users to formulate solutions to problems and then to test the consequences of their decisions (exemplified by the sophisticated challenges in multimedia games). Learners should be encouraged to make choices, take decisions and see the consequences of their actions, enter comments and information, attempt self-tests, and repeat activities to confirm their understanding. Opportunities for intuitive behaviour should be provided throughout the program.

For effective learning, the software should involve the user in both *intellectual and psycho-motor activities*. Keyboard use, mouse use (such as clicking, dragging, sliding and making a selection),

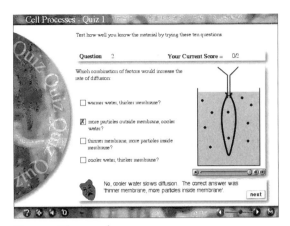

Figure 4. The use of supportive feedback to improve the learner's understanding.

reaction activities, etc, will help develop hand–eye–brain coordination, especially in young learners.

Providing regular opportunities for *self-assessment* is important for effective learning. To keep learners informed of their progress, regular embedded testing can be presented as an activity, challenge, quiz or game. These can take a variety of different forms, although particular forms may be repeated in larger programs to build familiarity. Although self-assessment should be non–threatening, a variety of devices can be used to enhance the challenge and engagement of the material, such as audio and visual responses (applause, animated characters), scoring points, working against the clock, variable degrees of difficulty, opportunities to repeat the activity and so on.

If the results of the activity are to form part of a formal assessment procedure, this should be made clear to the learner in advance.

Effective communication involves a two–way flow, and the importance of informative, clear and concise *feedback* is well documented in many fields of educational research. A well-designed multimedia program will provide feedback to learners in many different ways using text, audio or visual forms.

Wherever practicable, remedial feedback should be given. Feedback *must* be given for *all* responses to a multiple-choice quiz. Where a response is incorrect, the feedback should indicate the error, and provide some further information designed to help the learner realise why the answer was incorrect *(Figure 4)*. Negative or sarcastic comments should usually be avoided, but if it is crafted with skill and care, humorous feedback can be very engaging. A Review option can be beneficial, through which the source material upon which the question is based may be revisited for revision purposes.

Feedback takes many other forms, all of which are valuable in enhancing the learning experience.

Visual and audio feedback usually accompanies interaction with objects. Buttons (controls) often respond to being pressed by

Figure 5. The roll-over help at the bottom of the screen is context-specific.

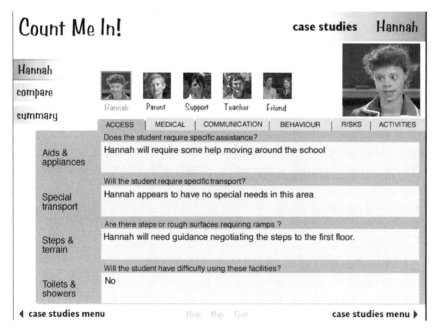

Figure 6. Tabs and an associated graphic surround used to indicate location.

moving and clicking.

A cursor that changes to indicate function is a subtle but valuable way of informing a learner about available options, such as "hot-spots", items that can dragged, images that can be magnified, and so on.

Alert sounds are often used to warn the user that they have made an error, such as hitting an inappropriate key or selecting an incorrect control. These are often accompanied by text feedback explaining the error and what should be done.

Roll-over help reveals the consequences of an action before it is taken. It takes different forms, including balloon help and message boxes *(Figure 5)*.

An indication of current selection – such as a highlighted tab or button, or a graphic device – is useful to remind the learner what decision has been taken.

An enhanced awareness of location can be achieved in a variety of ways, such as the graphic coding of backgrounds, the provision of menu subsections, or the use of icons representing place *(Figure 6)*. Unique screen names are often useful.

A visual indication of prior selection is a useful reminder of sections that have been completed, particularly in complex hierarchies or on screens with a number of jumping-off points. A common example is the changed colour of a Web link that has been activated.

Figure 7. Sophisticated Find tools allow the user to collate screens of interest.

A commonly-used and effective device is to use animation in feedback. For example, the next screen may appear to slide onto the current screen, enhancing a sense of physical movement within the program's structure.

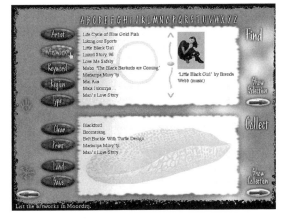

Simulations should provide feedback to the learner about the consequences of a particular action or decision. For example, if the simulation were of "throwing a basketball", the ball's flight could be traced on the screen, allowing the learner to reassess the situation, adjust the controls and try again.

Help screens explain different aspects of the program, such as navigation,

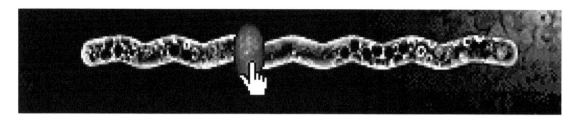

functions, structure and tools. Context-sensitive help (which tailors the information to suit the perceived need of the learner at that point) is particularly valuable, although its design presents significant challenges.

    Events should always be made explicit to the learner. Both audio and visual indicators can be used to show that something has happened.

Figure 8. The "Slider" — dragging the control scrolls through a set of screens.

Navigation

Movement through a multimedia environment (*navigation*) can be accomplished in many ways. However it is done, the user needs to clearly understand what has occurred. Navigation in a multimedia game environment can be an end in itself, but in a learning program, navigation should be a purposeful and unambiguous

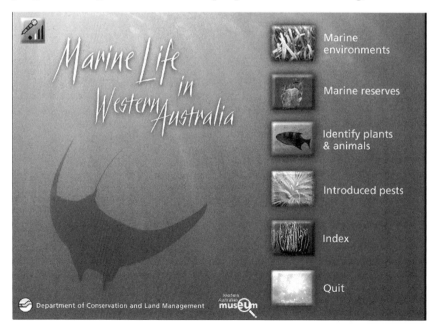

Figure 9. Full colour interfaces can establish the theme of the program.

means of moving through the information. Methods include:
- user–activated controls such as web links, arrows or other hot-spots;
- maps, which are useful not only to help the learner locate themselves within the material but as a means of navigation;
- automatic moves following the completion of a particular task eg. dragging an object to a microscope icon might move the user to an enlarged view.
- keyword searching–and–linking and Find tools that allow users to gather and view material via a word-search, or to forge links of their own and to examine information in a manner that suits their individual abilities. (See Figure 7) Location tools can be used by instructors or learners to blaze and save trails, to mark position (to return to, or for others to visit) and to backtrack.
- scrolling devices, that allow jumps through a list of screens. (See Figure 8).

Navigation should deliberately include redundancy, whereby there is usually more than one way to move to or locate material. A good search tool is flexible, and the available search criteria should match the user's needs. If it accepts user-input, the tool should be tolerant of missing or unknown values.

Navigation options enhance a learner's sense of control over the pace and direction of their activities. Although this may not directly increase achievement, a sense of control is likely to have its most significant impact on maintaining a learner's motivation, and in this way will influence achievement.

Interface Design

Given the possible range of media involved (text, audio, video, photography, graphics, etc) and the potential complexity of the structure and function of a multimedia program, interface design is of critical importance in providing an effective learning experience. A *graphic user interface (GUI)* is the most effective means developed to date to empower a learner to interface with a large information base. The interface should embody good graphic design, be consistent, and be designed to become rapidly familiar to new users *(Figure 9)*.

As far as possible, and so that the computer does not hinder the

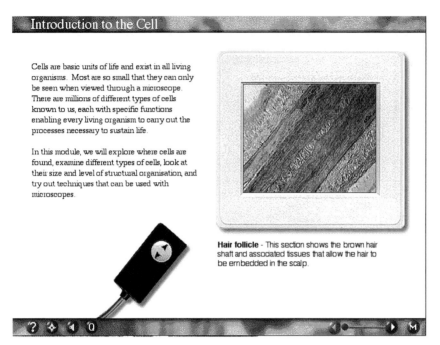

Introduction to the Cell

Cells are basic units of life and exist in all living organisms. Most are so small that they can only be seen when viewed through a microscope. There are millions of different types of cells known to us, each with specific functions enabling every living organism to carry out the processes necessary to sustain life.

In this module, we will explore where cells are found, examine different types of cells, look at their size and level of structural organisation, and try out techniques that can be used with microscopes.

Hair follicle - This section shows the brown hair shaft and associated tissues that allow the hair to be embedded in the scalp.

Figure 10. Balancing the visual elements avoids overwhelming the learner.

communication process between learner and information, the interface should be designed to be "invisible". It should have a minimum of on-screen clutter, and tools and controls should only appear when they are appropriate. Wherever possible, make everything obvious or intuitive. Some interfaces already use handwriting-recognition and voice-recognition to reduce the need for users to learn new skills to operate the technology. These, and over-the-horizon techniques such as gesture-recognition and eye-tracking, will all help to lower the obtrusiveness of the interface and enhance learning.

Standardisation and consistency are the keys to ease-of-use and rapid take-up. An excellent example has been set by the Macintosh graphic user interface that has benefited from a clear set of guidelines laid down for developers by Apple Computer.

Researchers have found that the layout of information on a printed page has an impact upon the effectiveness of learning, and there have been suggestions that screen layout should follow suit. The temptation to exploit the technical possibilities by crowding the layout has to be avoided. Unless a balance between the positive (information) and negative (blank space) areas of the screen is found, the layout will become dense, subtlety lost, and the message obscured *(Figure 10)*. Consistent and spacious layouts, achieved through restraint and a sympathetic appreciation of the needs of the learner, provide a sense of order and structure and facilitate the assimilation of information. An effective layout reflects the purpose of the instructional designer by making the activities to be undertaken on the screen apparent to the learner.

Effective screen design has much in common with the effective design of printed pages, and the fundamental rules of graphic design still apply. Factors such as unity, dominance, balance, weight, working to a grid, directing the eye around the screen, style, contrast, repetition, texture and composition are just as important in the electronic world *(Figure 11)*.

Graphic user interfaces often use *icons* that symbolise a function. The use of icons can significantly reduce screen clutter by replacing words – an icon of a printer can be interpreted more quickly and with less conscious thought than a box saying "Click to Print". But wherever icons are used, they should be designed and used with care, and they should be meaningful to all users. Roll-over help is useful in explaining function, especially for novices or

Figure 11. The 'Moorditj' program, with interfaces designed by indigenous Australian artists.

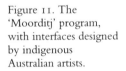

where the icons and functions are unusual.

The selection of appropriate fonts is an overlooked but extremely important element of building an effective, legible and engaging interface. Fonts that have been designed for their appeal on the printed page may have no place on the pixelated face of a computer screen. Designers are showing an increasing awareness of the value of fonts that have been purpose-built to be highly legible and attractive on the screen (such as those developed by Rosemary Sassoon)★★★. At the very least, interface designers should confine themselves to very few fonts per program, and should use coloured fonts sparingly and appropriately.

The use of the keyboard should be consistent, global controls should maintain the same design and should always be placed in the same position on the screen.

A sense of place

The obvious differences between the look-and-feel of an electronic document and the look-and-feel of a paper document have meant that some important qualities of the book, such as proximity and closure, are difficult to reproduce on screen.

Proximity is the capacity of a book to visually present related items in close proximity to one another, something that is difficult to achieve through the constraining medium of a computer screen. A sense of proximity can be promoted by drawing together like concepts as a series of *layers* on a single named screen, a metaphor familiar to users of graphics software. The learner explores the different layers of information, made aware that they relate to one another (see Figure 2).

Closure is the visual and tactile feeling through which the reader of a book becomes aware that they are approaching the conclusion. Where it appears important to convey closure to the learner, devices (such as the "Slider" in Figure 8) can be employed that indicate to the learner the scale of the sequence being explored, and the learner's current position in that sequence.

Conclusion

As I observed early in the chapter, we have a great deal to learn about the effective design of computer-based learning materials, and the rapid pace of technological change means that we are aiming at a moving target. But the technology must be kept in perspective – it is merely a means to an end – and much of what we know about learning holds true, regardless of the delivery mechanism. The educational media *"... are mere vehicles that deliver instructions but do not influence student achievement any more than the truck that delivers our groceries causes changes in nutrition. ... only the content of the vehicle can influence achievement"* (Clark). As the genre develops, we will learn a great deal more, but none of it is likely to overturn the basic tenets of informed and thoughtful design.

References
Clark, R.E. (1983). Reconsidering research on learning from media. *Review of Educational Research, 53,* 445–459.

Epilogue

So where are we going and what will be the result? Will the next generation be so dependent on their computer that other skills will atrophy? Will drawing by hand – either of letters, figures or whatever – become neglected and devalued? Probably not. These things tend to go in cycles, though this cycle may be a little different to those that came before. That is because technology is seen as the great time saver – the solution to all our problems. It will remain to be seen how deeply craftsmanship is embedded in the human character. For the creation of letterforms in whatever medium has been the province of the craftsman, not the technician, in the past.

However, the computer has allowed huge advances in typography as can be seen in some of the preceding chapters. Savings in time and labour that, allied to technological skill, have made complex projects possible and economical. This is true so long as we remember that the computer, however cleverly programmed, does not do the job without skilled direction, and that direction does not come without training and due deference to past expertise as well as modern wizardry.

There are things to balance here. It is possible that overuse of computers already means that our children are not developing their memories, and some of us worry that being able to access information at the press of a button will not mean the retension of that information but the further erosion of the faculty of memory. Is human memory becoming redundant? All this merits serious thought. Then we should acknowledge that the computer is governed by logic. Will that eventually program us to conform only to logic? It could be argued that logic is the antithesis of inspiration – and what are the implications of that for typography and creative thinking in general?

There are no answers to all this - only questions.

Index

Adobe Acrobat PDF
30,38,74,115,122
advertising 10,15,19
Aldus Pagemaker 65
alphabets 30,38,42,54,93,96
see also non-Latin scripts
American spelling 135
anamorphic scaling 112
see also characters, scaling
André, J. 98,115
animation 137
Apple 30,64,65,124,144
see also Macintosh
Arabic calligraphy 42,52
Arabic typography 46,48,52
Arial 30
arts and crafts 78,81-83,85-
87,148
arcade games
see computer games
arrows 18
audio-visual media
see multimedia
Autologic photocomposing
machines 99
authorship 76
autotracing 113

backgrounds 11,12
backtracking 143
banner advertisements 17
Baudin F. 22,40
Bengali 46-48
Berry, D.M. 104,116

bitmaps 100,101,104,114
blank lines 14
Bodoni G. 95
books
advantages of
25-27,129,136,137
design 68-70
difficulty in reading 22
future of 75,76
jackets 68-71,73
bold type 130
boxing text
36,126,129,130,141,145
Briem G.S. 8
brochures 10
see also advertising
Bullets 18

Caldwell, G.F. 88
calligraphy 42,48,52,75,77,95,97
see also handwriting
capitals 19,111,130
captions 10,13,17,128
Carter H. 102,115
cascading style sheets
26,31,36,37
casting off 71
cataloguing 76
CD-ROMs 124,133
cellular phones 77,78
characters
configuration 113-115
images 100,103,109,111-113
scaling 102,103,105,108,
109,111,112
shape definition 113
size
see typeface, size
spacing 73,84

stroke weights
   see stroke weights
Chartier, R. 76
children's needs
   118,119,121,130
Chinese characters 42,58
Clark, R.E. 147
closure, sense of 146
clutter 129,144
cognitive styles
   see individual differences
colour 128,129,137,141,142,146
column width 16,32
compositors 83,86
comprehension versus reading
   speed 121
computer
   alignment of initial letters 10
   CDs 124
   decline of writing 148
   effect on education
      84,118,119,125,132,147,148
   floppy disks 124
   games 8,11,125,142
   hardware manufacturers 122
   literarcy 126,134
   screen width 31,32
   typeface development
      see Colorado; Metafont;
        Postscript; Sassoon;
   TrueType
   typesetting 69
   typographic skills
      14,24,72,75,84
   versus handwriting 75
connections 134-136
content lists 18
context-sensitive help 142
   see also help screens

contour-based methods 113,115
contrast 128,130
control by learner 143
copperplate scripts 96
counter widths 101,102,110,111
crafts
   see arts and crafts
CSS
   see cascading style sheets
creativity 148
curves 111

dazzle 129
degradation, graceful 28,37
Desarmenien, J. 116
desktop publishing 22,52,87,127
Development Unit for Industrial
   Technology 131,133
Devangeri 46,48,52
digital type and typesetting
   64,113
Diringer, D. 54
discovery in learning 136
Dormer, P. 89
Dowding, G. 22,40
downloading 13
drawing
   continuous curves 108
   freehand 8,91,96,97,148
   importance of 96
   Industrial Revolution 96
   instruments
      85,96,104,105,108
   lettering design
      91,96,100,101,106,111-115
   Metafont 104
   technical 96,97
drop initials 10,18,19

DUIT
  see Development Unit for
    Instructional Technology
dust jackets
  see books, jackets
dvips 112
dyslexia 61

ECMAScript 36
education
  book design in 126,132
  computers,
    effect of 7,84,121
    lack of understanding of
      role of 132,147
  government policy 85
  graphic design 82-85,87
  importance of content 147
  IT teachers 125,126
  Japan 59,60
  learner control 138
  market 120,122,126
  software
    7,8,117,118,125,126,130,131
  special needs 125
  teacher training 126
  typography students 7,82
  working alone 85
  worksheets 126
e-mail 77,78
English,
  difficulty in learning 54
  see also spelling
engraving 95-97
error notification 141
etymology
eye
  critical faculties 95
  fatigue 8,22,128-130

hand-brain coordination
  79,97,139
  movements 127,144,145
  tracking 144

fax 77,78
feedback 139,141
feminism 78
find tools 143
fine arts 82
film setting 72
font producers
fonts
  see also typefaces
  choice 30,120,146
  interface design 146
  producers 113
  size 29
Fontographer program 113
foreshadowing 27,28,34

galleys 70,71
games
  see computer games
Geneva 30
gesture recognition 144
Gill E. 96
glossaries 136
Gonczarowski, J. 113,115
graphic design
  82,83,86-88,127,30,131
graphic user interface 143-145
graphics versus text 36
guided discovery 136
grids
  font design 100,101,
    106,108,109
  galleys 71
  layout 10,16,145

Gutenberg, J. 69
gutters 16

hand-eye-brain coordination
  138,139
hand skills 91,97
handwriting
  see also calligraphy
  book on typography 22
  influence of computers 75
  influence on Sassoon Primary
    120
  joined up 120
  letter design 91
  machine recognition 144
  manuals 77
  manuscripts 21
  printers' letterforms 7,91
  teaching 120
hardware manufacturers 122
Harvey, M. 8
headings and headlines
  10,17,18,130
help screens 141,142
Helvetica 18,30
Hersch R.D. 98
hierarchies 135,141
Hobby, J. 103,111
Hobsbawn, E. 97
Holland, J. 88
horizontal spacing 111
horseless carriages 132
hot-metal composition 46,64,72
HTML
  cascading style sheets
    26,31,36,37
  editors 37,39
  limitations
    23,26,31,34,38,122

Hughes, L.E. 121,131
hypertext linking
  Adobe Acrobat 38
  advantages 39,137
  colour 141
  informative text in 36
  navigation 35,137,143
  panels 122
  tables of contents 34
  text preferred to graphics 36
  to top of page 34
  to subheadings 34
  unpredictability 27

icons 128,145
ideographic scripts 55,56
Ikarus 113
illiteracy
  functional 54,55,60
  visual 97
illustrations and images
  attracting readers 8
  character
    see characters, images
  colour 129
  experiments with layouts
    68,73
  finding in books 27
  graphic links 36
  integration with text 70,129
  judging 97
  magnification 141
  mental images 8,134
  moving 137
  multimedia versus books
    136,137
  on screen 128,138
  text as graphics 33
Indian scripts 46,49

individual differences
133-135,137
Industrial Revolution 96
information
in relation to knowledge
134-136
initials 10,18,19
inspiration versus logic 148
instructional design 132,133,137
see also eduction
interaction 133,137-139
interface design
133,143,144,146
Internet
see also HTML; web
Japanese language 41,66
marketing 118
open-ended exploration 133
personal and business life 7
resistance to 7
interpolation algorithm 111
intranets 133
intuitiveness 144
invisibility 144

Japanese script 54,56,60
see also Kanji
JavaScript 36
Jeanes, R.J. 121
junk mail 10,11
see also advertising
Jury, D. 88
justification
Arabic script 48
short lines 128
Thai script 49
word spacing 128
young readers 128

Kana 56,58-61,64,65
Kanji 42,56,58-61,64,65
kerning 18
keyboards 49,55,146
keyword searching 143
Knuth D.E. 103-106,109,116
knowledge
in relation to information
134-136

laser image setters 98,100
laser printers 112
Lasker, M. 121
Latin alphabets
see also alphabets; non-Latin
scripts
types designed for 42
law 76
layers 146
layout
8,40,73,83,126,131,144-146
leading 26,29
learning
connections in 134,135
environments 133
individual differences 133-135
prerequisites for 133,134
problem-based 136
psycho-motor activities
138,139
readiness and motivation
134,135
self-assessment 139
user control 143
legibility
ascenders 130
classroom displays 129
colour 137
fonts 30,31,46,49,111

industrialised type 21
letterforms 129
newspaper classifieds 102
serifs 62
standards 7
tests 120,121
traditional views 74
versus novelty 74
web pages 22,24,27,28,
Letraset 84-86
letterforms
    alternatives 119
    Arabic 42
    Bengali 46
    common components 46
    development & construction
        95,97
    educational software 117,125
    handwritten 7,77,148
    Kanji 58,59
    legibility 129
    Letraset 84
    mental images 8
    use by artists 96
lettering arts 75,77,79,80
libraries 76,79
licences 122
ligatures 49
line lengths 14,22,31,32
line spacing 129
lines, blank 14
linguistics 87
Linotype 46,122
location tools 143
logic versus inspiration 148

Macintosh
    see also Apple versus Windows
        27,31,144

magazines 14,18
    see also newspapers
mail order brochures 10
    see also advertising
Malayalam 46
McLean, R. 22,40
Mandel L. 99-103,106,108,
    111,112,114-116
maps 143
market research 13
marketing 13,118,120-122,124
mass production 21,38,78
mechanisation 81,96-97
memory, human 148
Metafont 103-106,108,
    112,114,115
metaphors in multimedia 132
Meynell, F. 73
Microsoft 30
migrane 130
mobile phones 77,78
monitor size 16
Monotype 113,116,122
Moorditj program 145
Morris, R.A. 115
Mosley J. 97
motivation 134,143
mouse roll-overs 36,140,141,145
multilingual content and displays
    55,134
multicultural societies 53
multimedia
    audio and visual quality 138
    compared with the invention
    of printing 76
    definition 117,133
    feedback 139
    hierarchies 135
    individual differences 133,134

influence on learning
117,132,134,138,139
interface 143
interaction 138
navigation 142
redundancy 136
simulations 138
spatial and visual nature 137
structure and content 135,136
technological metaphors 132
typographical education 87
versus books 136,137

Nasta'liq calligraphers 48
navigation 16,32,34-36,122,
134,135,141-143
Netscape 26,36
New Age 78
newspapers 14,53,56,64,130
see also magazines
Nielsen, J. 39,40
non-Latin scripts 42,46,48,52
non-linear scaling
see characters, scaling

offset-litho process 62,71
open-ended exploration 133

page layout
see layout
PageMaker 65
paper, cost of 99
paragraph length 14,16
pens 77,79,95,97,104,105,108
see also drawing
phonetic scripts 56,58,59,60
photocomposition
46,49,64,99,114
photography 113,143

pictographic scripts
see ideographic scripts
pictures
see illustrations and images
pointing fingers 18,19
PostScript 49,100-106,109,
112,114,115
print runs, short 101
printed page versus screen
127,144,145
printers' roles 70,73,84
printing
education for 7,82-85,87
graphic design
36,82,83,86-88
history 42,76,95
proofreading and proofs
112,114
proximity, sense of 146
Pumfrey, P.D. 121
punchcutting 95-97,113

QuarkXPress 65,74
QuickTime 137
Qwerty keyboard 55,66

rasterisation 100-102,104,
105,109,114
readability
see legibility
Read, H. 82
reading
ability 121
difficulties
see illiteracy, functional
performance and speed 121
redundancy 136,143
religion 78,79
resolution 26

Riddle, J.R. 88
robots 115
roll-overs 36,140,141,145
Roman alphabet
    see Latin alphabets
rules of typography
    forgotten 86
    graphic design 145
    history 81
    individuality 92
    new 84
    position of radicals 61
    web font sizes 29

Sabon 30
Sassoon R. 121,146
    see also typefaces, Sassoon
scaling
    see characters, scaling
Schmoller, H. 70
screen clutter 128,144,145
screen fonts 146
screens versus printed page
    127-129,144,145
scrolling 13,27,32,143
sequencing 135
    see also navigation
sentence spacing 14
Seybold J.W. 100,116
Sheng, B. 42
Siegel, D. 24
simulations 136,141
Sinhala 49
slider 146
sounds,
    notification of errors 141
Southall R. 113,116
spacing
    characters 73,78

horizontal 111
leading 26,29
lines 129
on screens 128,129
optical and visual 21,128
paragraphs 14
sentences 126
single pixel gif 24
versus typography 21
vertical 111
word 21,128
spatial structure 128
special needs 125
spelling 55,59,135
Stamm, B. 115
Stone S. 7,116
stroke weights
    box margins 128
    Colorado 111
    inconsistency 100
    Kanji 66
    legibility 129
    Lumitype 109
    mixing different 103
    pixel counts 101,102
    PostScript 114
    proliferation of typefaces 96
    screen layout 145
    TrueType 102
    typographic parameters
        99,101
studio culture 87
subheadings 14,18
    see also headlines
subscripts and superscripts 49

tables
    graphics 33
    of contents 34,35

PDF 38
  text width 31
  web browsers 26,31,32,37
Tamil 49
technology, changes in
  20,75,76,118,132,147
telephone directories 98,99,122
  see also US West Dex
television 138
tests of legibility 121
TeX 112
text length 71
Thai 49
thumbnails 18
time-based phenomena 137
Times New Roman 30
Tracy W. 102,114,116
traditions
  apprenticeships 81
  asymmetric styles 70
  avante garde styles 70
  craft skills 78,82
  graphic designers' attitudes
    83
  Japanese 65
  liberating effect of computers
    68,69,73
  limitations in web
    environment 24,27,34
  matrix manufacture 113
  oral 48
  printer's role 70,73,84
  type vendors 118,121,122
  typefounderies 46
  typographic education 69
  value of 7
transfer lettering 71,84
TrueType 102,103,105
Twyman, M. 88,89

type
  designers & designs
    51,52,96,113
  founderies 96
  manufacturing systems 113
typefaces
  children's needs 118
    see also typefaces, Sassoon
  Clottes 101,103
  Computer Modern 106,109
  design 8,52,53,92,98,
    100-108,119
  feeling for 73
  for learning to read
    see Sassoon
  Helvetica 18,30
  Lumitype convention 109
  Montessori 120
  new 120
  piracy 53
  Sabon 30
  sans serif 31,62
  Sassoon 118,120-122,124
  size 10,18,26,72,100
  Times New Roman 18,30
  Verdana 30
  weight
    see characters, stroke weight
typing and typewriters 15
typographers, self-effacing 70
typography
  children's books 121
    see also typefaces, Sassoon
  distinguished from printing
    24
  education 7,69,82
  history 72,81
    see also technology,
      changes in

letterforms and other design
   factors 125
photocomposition 72
mass production 21
reading perforrnance 8
relationship to handwriting 7
rules
   see rules of typography
social and organisational
   change 70,71,73
technical change
   see technology, changes in
traditional skills and
   knowledge
      see traditions
web pages 11
typewriters 15

underlining 129
Unix 31
Urdu 48
US West Dex 98-103,106,
   108,112,114
user-friendliness 144

Verdana 30
vertical spacing 111
video 76,137,138,143
virtual reality 137
visual discomfort *see* eye fatigue
visual display units *see* screens
visual illiteracy 97
visual relationships 109,111,115
visually impaired readers 31
voice recognition 144

Walbaum 95
Warde, B. 70,83,88
web browsers 23,24,26,38

web multimedia capabilities,
   limited exploitation of
      137,138
web navigation
   see navigation
web pages
   access and readability 22
   attracting readers 10,11,17
   backgrounds 11,12
   downloading 13
   link colour changes 141,143
   printing 16
   scrolling 13
   size 13,27
websites
   design 87,122
   marketing 122
Wilkins, A. 121,122,129,131
Williams, A. 124
Wilson, F.R. 91,97
Windows versus Macintosh
   27,31,65
Wolpe, B. 70
word processing 22,23,38
word spacing 21,128
   see also spacing
Working Party for Typographic
   Teaching 87,89
writing
   see handwriting; calligraphy

XHTML and XML 34,39

Yanai, S. 104,116
Yeats, W.B. 75
Yakout 46

Zapf H. 8,92